trim healthy mama™

one hundred
DAYS OF INSPIRATION

A DEVOTIONAL FOR WOMEN OF ALL AGES & STAGES
THREE GENERATIONS OF FAMILY WISDOM

WELBY
STREET
PRESS

Clovercroft Publishing

One Hundred Days of Inspiration: A Devotional for Women of All Ages & Stages

Published by Welby Street Press, in association with Clovercroft Publishing, Franklin, Tennessee

Published in association with Larry Carpenter of Christian Book Services, LLC
www.christianbookservices.com

Cover Design by Trim Healthy Mama

Interior Layout Design by Suzanne Lawing

Edited by Gail Fallen

Printed in the United States of America

978-1-940262-45-1

All Scripture used in this book are from the King James Version or Revised Authorized Version. Other translations mentioned and abbreviated in the text are as follows:

CEB	Common English Bible
ESV	English Standard Version
GNT	Good News Translation
HCSB	Holman Christian Standard Bible
JBP	J. B. Phillips, The New Testament in Modern English
MSG	The Message
NASB	New American Standard Bible
NIV	New International Version
NKJV	New King James Version
NLT	New Living Translation
RSV	Revised Standard Version
TLB	The Living Bible
WEB	World English Bible

Dedicated to the memory of
Joyce Kathleen Bowen--
Mother, Grandmother, and
Great-grandmother of the authors.
A woman who loved God,
loved her home,
and loved her kitchen
where she spent hours preparing
healthy and nutritious food to delight
the tastebuds of all who entered.

Her Kitchen—A Psychiatry Office

"I learned by watching my Nana that the kitchen is more than just a room. Her kitchen had a heartbeat. There was more life there than at the local coffee house. It was there she welcomed friends and the lonely. An herb tea made in a pottery teapot and "something nourishing to eat" were the items on her menu during visiting hours, though there never seemed to be a closing time. But it wasn't just for the homemade food they came. It was the listening ear she offered and the well-chosen words of counsel. Her kitchen was not only a place to feed the hungry; it was a psychiatry office with a stool for a couch."

~ From "More Than Toast and Pots and Pans" by Pearl Barrett
(written about her grandmother)

Contents

INTRODUCTION

A Forever Vision

Because God has put eternity in our hearts (Ecclesiastes 3:11 ESV), we should also see life not only in the present, but also in the context of remembering past generations, and conscious of our influence upon future generations. We are not an entity unto ourselves. We are products of our forefathers and foremothers. How we live our lives today will affect our grandchildren, great-grandchildren, and yes, many generations to come.

Therefore it is a joy for us to write these inspirations to you from three generations and also influenced by a fourth generation, the great-grandmother who has now passed on. Her influence continues upon our lives and writings today.

Each one of us (Serene, Pearl, and Meadow) live close by one another and get to see one another nearly every day. I am also blessed that twenty-four of our forty-one grandchildren (so far) live nearby and also interact daily with one another. It is great life! As the young grandsons grow into young men, they "keep one another straight," according to their own words. It is a joy to see them not only growing up tall in stature (many of them are well past 6 feet tall) but also growing tall and strong in God.

When God first revealed Himself to Abram as the "Almighty God," He gave him an important message. However, He didn't give this message to Abram only, but to generations to come. In a few short sentences, God repeats five times that His Word and promises are to "You and your offspring after you" (Genesis 17:7-9 ESV).

I pray that our inspirations to you will set off a generational mindset in your heart. I pray that you will get a vision to live not only for your children today but also for their future families. God wants you to build a godly dynasty that continues down the generations.

We see God's plan when we read Isaiah 59:21 (ESV): "And as for me, this is my covenant with them," says the Lord: "My Spirit that is upon you, and my words that I have put in your mouth, shall not depart out of your mouth, or out of the mouth of your offspring, or out of the mouth of your

children's offspring," says the Lord, "from this time forth and forevermore.'"
It's a forever vision.

~Nancy

www.aboverubies.org

www.facebook.com/AboveRubiesUS

Physical and Spiritual

Many people try to lose a few pounds to fit into smaller jeans or to look great at their next class reunion. While there is nothing wrong with these goals, there is a much bigger picture to nutrition than merely looking a few months ahead. How you eat affects you not only now but also for decades in the future.

It impacts your children in utero, it affects their DNA and certain weaknesses toward diseases, and it influences their food habits (good or bad) for a lifetime. Our food choices also affect the way our children will teach their children and how their children will teach their children. We received our passion for health from our Nana, who passed it to our mother, who passed it to us.

However, we had more than health installed into us from past generations. We are so blessed to draw from a legacy of godly faith. Of course, as we grew up, we had to find, then walk out our own relationship with God, but we were nurtured from babyhood with Scripture and prayer as plentiful as our bread and butter.

We pass on the challenge to you to take up a baton of spiritual and physical health to those who come after you. Your pursuit in these areas will never be in vain. Future generations may be grateful that you took up this baton and imparted the precious truths you discover, just as we are grateful for our heritage.

~Serene and Pearl

www.trimhealthymama.org

www.facebook.com/trimhealthymama

Early in Life

Last night my grandparents invited me over for their weekly celebration dinner. After my Nana fed us with her home-cooked meal, my granddad fed us with God's meal. One of the courses was Psalm 63:1: "O God, thou art my God; early will I seek thee: my soul thirsteth for thee, my flesh longeth for thee in a dry and thirsty land, where no water is."

"What do you think 'early will I seek thee' means?" my Granddad asked.

"I think it means seeking early in the morning but also early in life," Nana answered. If we are to seek God early in the morning, then how much more important is it to seek God early in *life*?

Everyone's second birth story is unique and different. And just because someone was saved earlier in life does not always mean they are more righteous than those who were saved later in Life. But it is a burden for anyone to go that long without *knowing* Him. What we know before Him is doubt, fear, and sin. What a relief to grow up in faith, peace, and righteousness!

But not everyone has this privilege to seek Him early in life. A common reason is because of how they were *raised*. If all you were taught was the religion of evolution, you probably believed in evolution. If the parents you looked up to walked in sin, you probably followed their footsteps. If you grew up in a home without God, you were probably without God.

I was saved from this because I was saved *early in life*. My mom taught me (lessons learned from her mother, who was taught by *her* mother). Four generations walking in the light. Four generations drinking the water of life in the midst of a drought like Psalm 63:1 describes.

The first of these four generations was my Nana, Joyce Bowen. As Meadow Joyce Barrett, I was named after her. And while I was too young to remember her personally before she passed away, the acts of her life are echoed in my ears as she is praised like the Proverbs 31 woman by my family. She was a true lady who valued how God made her. She was a true heroine for influencing generations. I am honored to be named after her.

Never believe that seeking God is a chore; it is a delight. Never believe that a simple smile or daily task doesn't add to anything; it adds to much. Never believe that the way you live your life is only affecting you.

It is affecting generations.

~Meadow

One or the Other

We can confess one thing or the other. We can talk about the problems we are going through (which is what we usually tend to do), or we can choose to confess that God is with us.

God gives us a wonderful promise in Isaiah 43:2: "When you pass through the waters, I will be with you; and through the rivers, they shall not overflow you. When you walk through the fire, you shall not be burned, nor shall the flame scorch you." I hear many women confess how they are going through deep waters or a fiery trial. The problem is that when we keep talking about our difficulties, we end up staying under them.

Did you notice something in this Scripture? God promises that when we go through the deep waters, "I will be with you." When we are enduring the fiery trial, He says, "You will not be burned." That means we need to change our confession to "Father, I thank You that You are with me in this trial. You are bigger than this problem and I trust You!"

Your confession determines how you come through your trial. You can come out in victory or with the smell of the fire upon you. When you put your trust in the Lord, and confess *out loud* that God is with you, it will turn your heart from your problem to the Lord. You may still go through it, but you will go through it experiencing His power and presence with you.

~Nancy

Walk on the Water

What caused Peter to sink into the water in that famous story in the Bible? Doubt. He took his eyes off the Lord. Jesus called him to something that he would never have been able to do in his own strength. "Come." One simple word from Jesus, and Peter began to do the impossible. But then the wind howled and the waves tossed and Peter looked at his circumstances. He saw the strength of the storm and the weakness in himself.

Have you heard Jesus say, "Come?" Is He calling you to a healthier life, both physically and spiritually? But to get there you feel like you'll almost have to walk on water? Your past says you can't. Too many failures under your belt. And now the winds of doubt threaten to pull you under the waves.

Jesus was right there in the water with Peter. He wasn't calling from the shore. Just as Jesus did not leave Peter to drown but pulled him out of the waves and back into steps of faith, take the hand He is offering to you now. Today's a walking on the water day—even in the midst of a storm!

~Serene and Pearl

Why Me?

I have a medical condition called polycystic ovarian syndrome (PCOS). I could feel scared and sorry for myself. I could ask God why it's hard for me to stay at a healthy weight, while some of my friends can eat whatever they want and be skinnier than me. I could ask why I have to work twice as hard and only lose half as much weight as the average woman. Why me? Why am I at risk for cancer and diabetes if I am not extremely careful about how I feed my body.

Yes, I *could* feel that way. Maybe every now and then, those dark thoughts sneak up on me. Sometimes the spirit of fear that does not come from God whispers to me. I wonder if maybe the blood tests are wrong. Will my condition lead to infertility? What if I really do get cancer from this?

But most of the time, I feel the opposite. I shock people when I tell them the first feeling I got when I found out my diagnosis was excitement. Instead of looking at this condition as a crutch, I looked at it as a challenge to transform into a testimony. That thought excited me! God says to rejoice in our trials and tribulations. How can I relate to others who are struggling if I've never had a struggle myself?

When I first had to be strict about my lifestyle, it felt like a prison sentence. Instead of looking at all the things I could have, I looked at all the things I couldn't. But then I became thankful. I'm thankful I discovered my condition before it became something worse. I'm thankful I was no longer in the dark wondering what was wrong with me. Now, I look at others suffering around me and realize I am blessed.

~Meadow

two

Batten Down the Hatches

The number one vision of our lives should be to strengthen our marriage and family. Everything else must surrender to this priority. A child can be saved from much heartache later in life when brought up in a family where the father and mother love one another, are committed to one another, and have encouraged strong family ties.

Can I encourage you to strengthen your marriage a little more today? Ask God for something you can do today to make your marriage a little more lovelier, sweeter, and stronger. You may like to call your husband now to remind him that you love him.

What if you don't feel very loving toward him at the moment? Forget your feelings and do it by faith! And watch what will happen. Plan a delightful meal and have it ready for him as he walks in the door this evening. Write a love note to have waiting on his pillow as he goes to bed.

How many extra things are you doing outside the home this week? How many evenings are you going out? Why not cancel something and stay home with your husband and family instead? Think of a special thing you can do together as a family this evening. Turn off the TV and read a story together. Or get each family member to tell a story, read a poem, put on an act, or do something fun. You and your husband will be the audience, but be ready; the children will want you to perform something too!

Batten down the hatches! In other words, close your doors to the outside and shine the warmth of God's sunlight on the inside. Build up your family life rather than things outside of your family.

~Nancy

Gently Does It

Isaiah 40:11 says, "He gently leads those that are with young." Is our daily mindset to do our body good or harm? Hold on before you answer, "Good, of course." Harm is often disguised by culturally acceptable extremes. Many of us punish our bodies to get to a certain goal. Are you an abusive owner of your body, literally "whipping" it into shape with harsh prodding, merciless pushing, or cruel purging? What are the reasons? To atone for the french fries? To beat your body's imperfections? To try to live up to your own perfectionist standards? Or because magazine covers tell us to shred, cleanse, detox, cut and burn, and to push through the pain?

Gentle cleaning foods like lots of greens and adequate fiber should be a natural part of the diet. So should adequate exercise. But when the cleanse and purge mentality overtakes the build and nourish mentality, you might be in a state of imbalance. If you are a mother of little ones, this especially applies to you. Gentle up.

"I put in two hours at the gym" is celebrated in our culture with a "You go, girl!" It is common for people to begin their New Year with a week of drinking nothing but juices. Sadly, this often leads to the cycle of binging and purging again. It's a January trap.

The lifelong gentle road with overall healthy habits that are not obsessive or cruel is a much happier and healthier way to live.

~Serene and Pearl

From Challenge to Change

When I was around fifteen, my mom encouraged me to be active, but I hated working out with a passion. I was no longer that energetic little girl who'd run around and play outside. Being homeschooled, I missed out on PE and sports, so I started exercising at least three times a week for my physical education. This would be my new healthy habit, Mom decided. Still, working out was the least favorite part of my education.

It's something everyone should do for life. For life? For life! I couldn't believe I had to do this dreadful thing for (gulp) . . . life. Surely, when I graduate from high school, I'll graduate from this, right?

Interrupting the past with the present, I've graduated school now and

I work out now more than ever. It's not something I make myself do. It's something I want to do!

So how did I come to embrace what I used to despise? I incorporated one my passions (music) into my daily workout, and it turned a pain into a pleasure.

I put my earphones on and play one of my favorite songs. I walk and run until the song's finished, excited to hear the next song. At the end of my workout, I'm out of breath and hardly realize it because I'm so enjoying myself! What was once a chore can become a challenge, and what was once a challenge can become a change!

~Meadow

three

The Price of Greatness

When a new baby is born and we take this precious life into our arms, we are not only overcome with awe and delight but also the enormity of the task that lies ahead. We are responsible to keep this little life alive. We have to nurse, nourish, love, protect, and train our children until they one day leave our home. Even then, we never stop praying for them. Even then, their trials and challenges are still our concerns.

I remember more than sixteen years ago when Serene's oldest son, Arden, was born. A few days after his birth, he came down with the respiratory syncytial virus (RSV), and we had to rush him to the hospital. As baby Arden was turning blue, Sam, the new father, frantically asked, "How do we keep him alive?"

However, it is not only caring for a new life. Mothers bear the weight of managing a home and family. It's not like other careers where you clock in and out at a certain time. We feel this weight upon us *continually*.

Sir Winston Churchill once said, "The price of greatness is responsibility." Yes, you have great responsibility upon you, mother, but that's because your career is *great*, not because it is insignificant. Don't try to minimize the greatness of your career and relegate it on the sidelines. Embrace it fully. Embrace the responsibility. It is the price of greatness.

~Nancy

Inspired by True Beauty

Proverbs 17:22 says, "A merry heart doeth good like a medicine but a broken spirit drieth the bones."

Recently, we had to spend several hours at an airport in one of the biggest cities in the U.S. People watching passes the time, but we couldn't help noticing two extremes. Some women were so polished and perfect in their appearance, it was apparent their physical image was of utmost importance. Hey, we're not judging the effort to look nice; we should all put our best face forward. But many women walking past our spectator seats seemed heavily burdened with an impossible level of refinement—shoes, purse, nails, jewelry, hair, and face all buffed, polished, and shined to stunning perfection. Many wore a tight smile or remained expressionless.

On the other extreme, some appeared to have given up on their appearance, dragged down by life and health issues—frowns and despondency carved deeply into faces. Sloppy T-shirts, baggy sweats, and "I'm too far gone to change" written clearly on their countenance.

And then . . . a radiant elderly woman walked past. There were wrinkles on her face, but they comfortably housed the smile she beamed at Serene's baby. She couldn't help stopping to squeeze a chubby baby thigh. Purse and shoes did not perfectly match, but this was true beauty—an essence of youth even in her mature years.

We are in our late thirties and mid-forties. It's easy to fall into the false mindset (especially when you are in the public eye) that you have to look young, perfect, and polished. This is a lie. God has given us seasons of life, and all His seasons are precious and planned. We are both determined to smile more and concern ourselves less with perfection and youth.

~Serene and Pearl

Throw an Endurance Party

We might be struggling physically, others are struggling financially. Some are struggling emotionally or spiritually. If we feel like we're struggling alone in the ways of food, it doesn't mean we're the only ones suffering in this world! Everyone struggles. And if it wasn't yesterday, it's today. If it's not today, then it's tomorrow. It's all a part of our growing time here on earth.

Romans 5:3–5 says, "Not only so, but we glory in tribulations also: knowing that tribulation worketh patience; and patience, experience; and experience, hope: and hope maketh not ashamed; because the love of God is shed abroad in our hearts by the Holy Ghost which is given unto us."

Instead of throwing ourselves pity parties, let's throw ourselves endurance parties!

~Meadow

A Beautiful Word

One of the most beautiful Hebrew words in the Bible is *ta' anuwg*. It means "delightful, lovely, precious, cherished, pleasant, fondled." This word is used in three different ways to describe family life:

1) **The love of a husband and wife.** In Song of Solomon 7:6 (NLT), the husband says to his wife, "Oh, how beautiful you are! How pleasing my love, how full of delights!" Why is she so delightful? Because she takes time and thought to make herself delightful and desirable to her husband.

2) **A mother's love for her children.** In Micah 1:16 (ESV), God calls them "the children of your delight." Our children are to be "loved," "cherished," and "fondled." They are too precious to give to someone else to care for, aren't they? We treasure them enough to take this responsibility ourselves.

3) **A woman's love for her home.** Micah 2:9 (ESV) says, "The women of my people you drive out from their delightful houses." God was angry with those who would evict women from "the homes they love" (GNB). It is inherently within us to love our home. It is how God created us. Adam was created before God created the Garden of Eden, but He had the home waiting for Eve (Genesis 2:7, 8; 2:18-22).

And what did God call His first home? Eden means "delightful." God wants us to make our homes delightful—a delightful place for His presence, for our husband, and for our children. And why would we want to leave our delightful homes? Why would we forsake something we love for something lesser?

~Nancy

Blessed to Be Unique

We received an email from a woman who had finally reached her goal weight with THM. She was happy to see the number on the scale and to fit back into her wedding dress, but her joy was dampened. She asked us what we thought were the best exercises to reduce her thighs, which she thought still looked too big and out of proportion to the rest of her body. We replied that nice rounded thighs are a beautiful mark of womanhood and if she has achieved a healthy goal weight, why reduce them?

We are all shaped differently. Some women want more rounded thighs; they deal with rounded bellies while their thighs stay stick thin. Some women would love bigger breasts; others consider paying for a breast reduction. When will we be happy . . . accepting?

Our unique goal weights are completely different to someone else's; what the scale reads will be different as well. Both of us, for example, are at goal weights. Even though we are both tall, there's a difference of fifteen pounds between us, and we buy different- sized jeans. You can't exercise away your DNA—we are all unique, wonderful creations. Romans 9:20 (NIV) asks, "Does the clay say to the potter, 'Why did you make me like this?'"

~Serene and Pearl

Shining My Light

I experienced one of our nation's biggest, flashiest, liveliest cities earlier this year. When asked how I enjoyed it, I explained that I had two very strong emotions. The first emotion was that my mind was overwhelmed that there was so much to do. My eyes constantly shifted to be able to see all the sights. I was excited. I was thrilled. I was amazed. The second emotion was that I was getting the wrong vibes . . . bad vibes. I wanted to go home. No, not just go back to my earthly home, but to my heavenly home. I didn't even know if I wanted to live in this world if it was all like this.

We will have moments of fun and happiness in this life, but times are getting darker. Once I was back home, I realized that it's not just that big city I went to that's full of evil; there are struggles, sadness, and sin everywhere. I can barely go anywhere without being exposed to it. To Christians, this may make us want to escape the world itself. But that's the wrong mindset.

Yes, we are to flee sin (see 2 Timothy 2:22 and James 4:7). We are to flee so that we won't sin. We are to flee the ways of this world. But we are not to flee *from* this world. Why do you think God put us here? What else is our purpose on earth but to be lights?

~Meadow

five

Marriage Destroyer

One of the biggest stumbling blocks in a marriage relationship is pride. Pride reveals itself when we are stubborn and not willing to yield. It rears its ugly head when we stay on our "high perch" or keep our "high look" and are not prepared to humble ourselves.

Conversely, one of the greatest building tools in establishing a happy and sweet marriage is to have a humble and contrite heart. We certainly don't have this in our own flesh, but as we yield to the Holy Spirit, He works it in our hearts. And you will have the favor of God upon you. When you have God's favor on your marriage, you will enjoy all kinds of wonderful blessings.

Over and over again God reminds us that He hates pride. Psalm 101:5 (NIV) says, "Whoever has haughty eyes and proud heart, I will not tolerate." The CEB translation says, "I can't stomach anyone who has proud eyes or an arrogant heart." Wow! God runs from pride! We won't experience His presence anywhere near us when we keep our proud heart (see James 4:6 and 1 Peter 5:5).

But whom does God want to dwell with? Those who have "a contrite and humble spirit" (Isaiah 57:15). When we follow the example of Jesus and humble ourselves, God comes right into our marriage with His mighty presence, melting stubbornness, softening hardness, and turning our hearts to one another.

~Nancy

Which Voice?

Serene: *My four-year-old, Breeze, has two names for people, "nic-ey" and "meanie." Meanies are people who do not cater to her every whim, but that's another story. Pearl and I were chuckling at her "nic-ey" or "meanie" names for her brothers and sisters and realized these two characters exist in our minds and talk to us all day long.* ❦

We have meanie thoughts and nicey thoughts. We can choose which thoughts to make friends with and which to reject. If all of our thoughts were truthful and uplifting, there would be no need for the Scriptures to encourage us to filter out the meanies. A great example is in 1 Peter 1:13, which reminds us to "Gird up the loins of your mind."

The meanies tell you it can't be done, that it's too hard. They say you won't stick to it, and if you mess up, there's not much use jumping back to a commitment. They say you're washed up and there is no use trying. They say you are not special, you are not pretty, you are not important, and there is no hope.

What do we do about these meanies? Don't make a nice, furnished apartment for them in your mind. Don't feed them or they'll stick around. When they whisper, fight back with the truth. Psalm 139:14 says, "I am fearfully and wonderfully made." Philippians 4:13 says, "I can do all things through Christ who strengthens me." And Jeremiah 29:11 says, "For I know the plans I have for you, declares the Lord, "plans to prosper you and not to harm you, plans to give you hope and a future."

~Serene and Pearl

Practice Happy Thoughts

Sadness often leads to depression because our brain creates pathways. If we keep that sadness up for a long time, it will become our normal, trapped way of thinking. To reverse this effect, practice happy thoughts. Once you practice long enough, it will become natural.

Happiness leads to thought freedom!

~Meadow

six

To Serve or Not to Serve

I have been thinking about our great role of "serving" in womanhood. As a young mother I remember thinking, "I'm just a servant around this place." I was filled with selfishness and although I loved my children and loved motherhood, I still wondered why I had to be the servant.

As the years have moved on, I realize more and more that it is a privilege to serve. It is innately in us as women. We only reject it because of our selfishness, and in the end we miss out. God blesses us when we serve. We are fulfilled when we serve. We were born to serve.

Of course, we all want to "serve the Lord." That's our greatest ambition in life. Many mothers feel as though they are "stuck" with their children and can no longer serve the Lord. This is a lie. When you mother your children and pour your life into making your home a sanctuary for God, your husband, your children, and all who come in to your home, *you are serving the Lord!* This is your service to Him.

Psalm 100:2 tells us to "Serve the Lord with gladness." This means with "exceeding joy." The one who serves will be blessed. Don't expect to be waited on. Be happy to serve. Even Jesus, the Son of God, "did not come to be served, but to serve, and to give his life" (Matthew 20:28).

~Nancy

Breath of Life

Something so simple as breathing can have a huge impact on your health and energy levels. Take a moment and become aware of how you are breathing. Don't worry, this is not some New Age exercise. Some of us have such slumping postures that our lungs cannot draw in oxygen to full capacity.

Others of us take shallow, strangled, tight breaths due to stress. Sometimes, the stressful situation passes, yet the habitual tight breathing remains.

Stand up straight in a confident manner, imagining a string tied to the back of your head gently pulling you out of a slump. In this alignment, your diaphragm (housed in your lower ribs) can act like a bellow and draw in plenty of air to oxygenate your brain and body. Now take a breath. Feel your lower ribs gently expand as you draw in air.

Throughout the day if you feel tired, stressed, worried, or depressed, take a moment and just breathe in this manner. Breathe all the way in, then all the way out comfortably. Breathing like this will not change your circumstances, but it can help the way you react to them. Remember, breath is life!

~Serene and Pearl

It's Worth the Fight

If you're like me, you have a very stubborn body that fights as hard to keep its weight as you do trying to lose it. I'm dealing with PCOS and it seems that both my body and my willpower are as equally stubborn. As a result, they usually end up in a tie. I don't gain weight and I don't lose weight. I maintain weight.

I don't usually get anywhere, and it can seem hopeless. Sometimes, I wonder if I should just give up. But that's the wrong mindset. If I don't fight to at least *maintain* my weight, my situation could be worse. It could always be worse! And it's always worth the fight.

~Meadow

Most Fears Are Lies

We must be always be on guard against fear. There is a healthy fear that God gives us for our preservation and safety. However, we are often plagued with unhealthy fears, which come from the enemy. One of Satan's greatest ploys is to tyrannize you with fear. Not realistic fears but *unrealistic* fears.

Psalm 53:5 says, "There they were in great fear where no fear was." The literal meaning is "They feared a fear!" This is what Satan wants you to do. Fear a fear! And he is good at getting you to do that. Job 15:21 says, "The sound of fears is in his ears." This is not a true fear; it's only the sound of fear—the suggestion of what *might* happen!

Remember, God does not give you a spirit of fear, but of power and of love and of a sound mind (2 Timothy 1:7). Don't give into the phony doubts and fears the devil puts into your mind. He especially loves to put fears in your heart about having another baby. Or wondering how you could ever provide for another baby.

Fear stops you from doing the will of God. That's why the enemy uses fear against you. It immobilizes you. Debilitates you. Paralyzes you. Instead, fill your mind with God's Word. His truth *liberates* you!

~Nancy

That Was Yesterday!

"His compassions never fail. They are new every morning; great is thy faithfulness" (Lamentations 3:22, 23 NASB).

If God doesn't keep a record of wrongs, neither should you. He brightens the sky with a brand new sunrise every morning.

Today you have the opportunity to make fantastic health choices. Don't hold on to yesterday's mess—it is gone—ancient history, baby!

Our mother taught this poem to all of us six children. (Funny bit of trivia: she taped the words to the bathroom wall—or as we say down under, the loo.) Now we teach it to our own children.

> Two little men stood looking at a hill,
> One was named Can't and one was named Will,
> Can't said, "I never in the world can climb this hill,"
> So there he is at the bottom of it still.
> Will said, "I'll get to the top because I will."
> Two little men are living at the hill.
> At the bottom is Can't, at the top is Will.

What is your confession today? Whether your hill be one hundred pounds to lose, type 2 diabetes to beat, shedding the last stubborn ten pounds, or a sweet tooth that keeps pulling you back to your knees, you can choose to be Can't, or you can choose to be Will. There is a climb up that hill. You can't sail up it without effort, but keep on climbing!

~Serene and Pearl

Can't or Will

I grew up with the poem "Two Little Men." My mom used to tell it to my brothers and me when we were really young. I can picture the memory now: We're at the bottom of that long steep hill. We're staring up at it. It was fun to walk down, but here comes the hard part—walking back up. And my brothers and I are already feeling tired.

"I can't, Mom!"

But my Mom wouldn't accept any complaints. She told us about Can't and Will.

Sometimes the path to health seems like a very steep hill. And we get tired just thinking about it. But we will . . . we will climb that hill! Because we get nowhere if we say we *can't*.

~Meadow

eight

The Marriage Song

God has planned for us to live in joy. He equates weddings with joy. He associates motherhood with joy (Psalm 113:9). He relates fatherhood with joy (Psalm 127:5).

When Psalm 78:63 talks about God's judgment upon Israel, it says, "Their young women had no marriage song." We understand as we read this that God equates marriage with singing and celebration. The actual word in the Hebrew is "halal" which means "to celebrate, praise, shine, and to give in marriage." The word is mainly used in the Bible to praise the Lord. I love to be at weddings where there is exuberant singing and worship to the Lord, don't you? I feel sad when I go to a wedding and there is no singing. How can you celebrate without singing?

God loves to see and hear singing, praise, and joy at a wedding, when two people are united together to begin another family. God rejoices and we should rejoice. When God speaks of the blessing of God on the land, He talks about "The voice of joy, and the voice of gladness, the voice of the bridegroom and the voice of the bride, the voice of them that shall say, Praise the Lord of hosts" (Jeremiah 33:11).

When there are no marriages to celebrate—feasting, joy, and the marriage song—we are experiencing the judgment of God (Jeremiah 7:34; 16:9; 25:10; and Revelation 18:23). If you are planning a wedding, plan wedding songs of joy and celebration. And if you are married, keep the *marriage song* alive in your marriage.

~Nancy

Where Are My Beautiful Sheep?

"Where is the flock that was given to you, your beautiful sheep?" (Jeremiah 13:20 NKJV). These words leapt in my heart. They didn't feel stern, but more like a gentle prodding from the Chief Shepherd to a little shepherdess. It made me take a deeper assessment of my little flock.

It is not enough for me to make sure their teeth are brushed, their lessons are learned, their tummies are full, and they're tucked safe in bed at night. To what drum are their hearts beating? Is it the rhythm of the world, or are they in sync with the percussion of Heaven and the God of all creation?

Where are my beautiful sheep? Watched over by cartoons? Too many hours under the spell of iPhone games while I am distracted by less important day fillers?

You may not have children under your roof, but if you are a woman, you have a mother's heart and have been given one or more sheep to nurture. A friend, a co-worker, a neighbor, a niece or nephew—a flock can come in many different varieties and ways.

Do we have an eternal vision for our beautiful flock?

~Serene

Standing Straight

"God does not care for wimps," noted one of my favorite preachers. He was speaking in reference to how Ezekiel fell before God. But God would never give His message until Ezekiel was back on his feet!

At times when we ask God to help us get through our troubles, we act like helpless wimps before Him. It's true that we must be dependent on God. But even in helpless situations, we need to be courageous enough to hear and obey what He says.

And if you want to go the second mile, I have one of those families that is all about practicing posture. Not only does a good posture make us look better, it makes us look bold. Not only should we stand up for God, we should stand up straight.

~Meadow

·········· nine ··········

God Will Come

Are you waiting to hear an answer from God? Don't give up. Keep waiting. Keep *patiently* waiting. God will come to you in His time, not yours. But He will come. Do not doubt it.

In Psalm 40:1, David testifies, "I waited patiently [the Hebrew means "in waiting, I keep on waiting"] for the Lord; and He inclined unto me, and heard my cry." The word "incline" literally means "stretch down to." A number of translations say, "He bent down to me." Others say, "He stooped down to me." Isn't that wonderful? The Sovereign God of the universe hears your continual cry and stretches down from Heaven to deliver you.

David tells us what God did when He bent down to him: "He brought me up also out of a horrible pit, out of the miry clay, and set my feet upon a rock, and established my goings. And he hath put a new song in my mouth, even praise unto our God: many shall see it, and fear, and shall trust in the Lord" (Psalm 40:2, 3). No matter how horrible the pit you are in, it's not too deep for God to stretch down to you. His deliverance is so great, that He not only gives you a song to sing but a song that everyone can "see," and it causes them to trust the Lord.

~Nancy

Move in Him!

Acts 17:28 says, "In him we live and move and have our being." While we caution against over exercise, let's not be stagnant. God created our bodies to move. It is a disservice to him to let them rust and ruin through sedentary habits. We should relish times of rest and cuddly evenings on the couch with our loved ones, but if sitting is the standard throughout our day, our body will not function with the optimal blood flow and energy God designed for us.

No, you don't have to put in an hour on the treadmill, but do something more time effective that gets your heart rate up and works your muscles about three to four times a week. Muscles deteriorate without use and they are crucial for a healthy metabolism and overall health.

Take a brisk walk or even a leisurely stroll every day if you can. Weather does not always cooperate, so how about dancing around the living room with your children to music in the afternoon? If you are stuck in an office, get up every half hour and get your blood moving with simple stretches. No need to perform an Olympic gymnastics routine for your coworkers, but ten subtle body squats behind your desk can make a world of difference. "Oops, I have to pick up that pen for the tenth time . . . strange that I keep dropping it." Stand up at your desk if you can for a while to stretch your legs.

In fact, we've been writing at this computer all morning. Outside, here we come!

~Serene and Pearl

Are You Following?

Many Christians seem to think that it doesn't really matter if you make a commitment to study God's Word so long as you've accepted Christ as your Savior. But "Christian" means "Christ follower." How can you be a Christ follower if you don't follow Him? If you don't stay in His Word, which keeps the fire going, you won't have that longing to follow Him when the fire goes out.

~Meadow

.... ten ....

Waiting with Expectancy

What possibilities lie in the newborn babe! He is like a ship sailing out into the sea of life. There will be calm sailing with plenty of adventures and storms along the way. As parents, we teach him to know and trust his Captain and to understand the ways of the sea.

The newborn is like a little plant waiting to be nurtured, watered with prayer and God's Word, and filled with big doses of encouragement in order for him to grow into a mighty oak that will bring shelter and blessing to many people.

The newborn is like an unwritten book. God has the story already written, but He waits for the child to write on the blank pages. With much prayer, godly wisdom, and teaching, the parents guide him as he writes the story.

The new baby is like a precious jewel, waiting to be cut and polished so he will shine more and more brightly as he walks in this world. He will not only shine in this world, but Daniel 12:3 tells us that those who turn many to righteousness will shine "as the stars forever and ever."

Every new life is another revelation of the image of God in this world. Each new life comes with the potential to shed God's light into the darkness and destroy the works of the enemy. The child is not a life to itself. He will influence everyone he meets. Many more lives will be born as future dynasties come forth from this one child and shape generations to come. No wonder the devil hates new life!

~Nancy

Put Exercise in Its Place

In 1 Timothy 4:8, we learn: "For bodily exercise profiteth little but godliness is profitable unto all things, having promise of the life that now is, and of that which is to come." This Scripture does not say exercise is useless, but it does give us some context on how much emphasis to place on it. Also, the time when this Scripture was written was much more physically demanding than our modern and sedentary push-button lifestyles. Therefore, bodily exercise may profit *some of us modern folk* a bit more. When Paul wrote this Scripture, there was a lot of worship of the human form in Greek culture. He knew this pursuit of bodily perfection was a trap.

We also have to weigh this Scripture with others. The Proverbs 31 woman strengthened her arms and planted a vineyard.

So let's give a little part of our time to exercise to maintain physical fitness. Fifteen to twenty minutes of vigorous training three to four times a week qualifies as "a little." One to two hours for six to seven days a week is a lot! Of course, our days should not be sedentary, and we can stay active with our children, gardening, hiking, walking, playing sports . . . but this is just fun life, not specific training.

If you are giving a lot of your day and a lot of your thoughts to exercise, then according to this Scripture, you're wasting your life on temporal, surface ambitions. This body is just our tent; we do want to keep it in good condition so we can carry out God's will for our lives, but we repeat . . . it's just our tent!

~Serene and Pearl

Tough Love

I think parents are one of the greatest examples of tough love, especially loving parents. They know that without discipline and rules, their child might grow up selfish or become a criminal. They also know that *with* discipline comes hurtful feelings and misunderstandings. But they hope that when their child is older, they will look back and thank them for always steering them in the right direction.

I think that the Father in Heaven is the greatest example of tough love. His love can be tender, but He knows that without discipline and commandments, we will fall prey to our sinful nature and lose our souls. There are many who misunderstand God. He wants us to understand that every trial and tribulation we go through is for our own good.

We should be grateful to our parents now that we look back and understand their tough love. And we should be grateful to our Father in Heaven. Even if we fail to understand the reason for tough love now, we know He is the definition of love.

~Meadow

·········· eleven ··········

You Are Crowned

Have you ever worn a crown? Yes, you have, perhaps without realizing it! Psalms 103:1–3 says, "Bless the Lord, O my soul . . . who crowns thee with lovingkindness and tender mercies." Every morning God puts a crown on your head of His lovingkindness and tender mercies. Thank Him for this beautiful crown, and be consciously aware of wearing it as you walk through this day. It will change your attitude and turn your heart to God in gratitude and awe.

The Hebrew word "lovingkindness" is *chesed*, one of the most beautiful words in the Bible. It describes God's unfailing love and mercy to undeserving sinners and translates to "grace" in the New Testament, which can be understood as "God's riches at Christ's expense."

Psalm 103 gives us more understanding. Verse 8 tells us that God *abounds* in lovingkindness. Verse 11 says that God is *great* in lovingkindness, and verse 17 says that His lovingkindness is from "*everlasting to everlasting* upon them that fear him, and his righteousness unto children's children."

As God crowns you, why don't you crown others around you today with kindness and mercy?

~Nancy

What If You Hate Exercise?

To say that I am not athletic is an understatement. The last kid waiting to be picked for a team—yeah, that was me. I don't have a lot of natural muscle tone, I don't like to sweat, my base nature is to be lazy, and I don't get any sort of strange joy from the pain of muscles burning. I have never—

not once in my forty-three years—bounced out of bed and thought, "Exercise . . . oh goodie!" But I know it is good for me. It's necessary if I want to stay peppy and prevent the sagas of age . . . so I do it and do it regularly.

If you're like me and do not have any natural love for exercising, here are my tips:

1. Find something you hate the least.

I hate lifting heavy weights—that's out. I do not enjoy swimming—out. Cycling? Umm, no . . . out. That sounds hot. I *detest* running—out. But I do enjoy walking. In fact, I'd go as far as to say that I feel a sort of love for it. But a stroll is not really enough to combat sarcopenia (muscle wasting as we age). I love to stroll through our woods, but I don't count that as a workout. So I do sprint walking, which is simply periods of slower walking combined with all-out speed walking up hills. That counts!

2. Make your workouts manageable.

I know I can work out if the session is less than 20 minutes. Any longer, and I may not be able to convince myself it is worth it. I do short workout DVDs that focus on toning my body and increasing my heart rate. Check out our "Trim Healthy Mama Workins" DVD. It is actually . . . almost . . . dare I say it . . . fun!

3. The time of day counts.

If I had to work out as soon as I woke up, I might have to give up exercise forever. I'm a "give me coffee and leave me alone" person for the first hour or two of my day. Vigorous movement is not part of that time! I feel sufficiently wide-awake by about 9:30 a.m., so I usually exercise midmorning. But we're all different. What is your "doable" time of day?

4. Don't overdo it.

My goal for this sort of vigorous exercise is four times a week. Some weeks I only make it to three times, but I don't get down on myself for that. Life happens. I also take five days off around my cycle each month.

Despite my loathing of exercise, I have been able to do it faithfully this way for two decades now!

~*Pearl*

Would We Save the Body and Not the Soul?

We are not called to condemn. But we are called to warn.

If we saw a blind man walking into a burning house, would we warn him? Of course we would. We wouldn't keep quiet because we worry we might offend him! If we saw a spiritually blind man walking into a fiery furnace, would we warn him? Not everyone would. They worry they might offend him. But the man's very soul is in danger! They would save the body but leave the soul?

If we are the only chance to warn a blind soul, but we don't try . . . then the fault is ours.

~Meadow

twelve

Who Knows Best?

I recently read that 47 percent of Christian women do not believe we should put emphasis on the roles of marriage and motherhood. I beg your pardon? What has happened to our Christian society that they no longer think like the Bible? In the first few chapters of Genesis, God establishes His plan for mankind, which includes both marriage and motherhood.

I know that not all women will marry, but some of the greatest examples of mothers in our world are women who never married or bore children. We immediately think of Mother Theresa, Corrie Ten Boom, Gladys Aylward, Mary Slessor, Amy Carmichael, and the list goes on of women who embraced their motherly anointing. They poured out their lives to nurture and mother the hurting and needy, and in turn, were totally fulfilled women.

God only made two species of humankind—male and female. He didn't make two Adams to both do the same job. That would have been superfluous. He gave male and female a different assignment each, and they both fit together perfectly. If we are female, we should seek to embrace our "femaleness." To do anything else is a waste of our life. The more we reveal our femaleness, the more we give glory to God our Creator.

Let's be fully whom God created us to be.

~Nancy

Free Yourself from Obsessive Exercise

Unlike my sister, "Princess Pearlie," who hates to sweat and get uncomfortable, I actually love intense exercise. Yes, it hurts and burns and I feel like giving up sometimes, but I dig the challenge and the honing of new skills. I don't mind lifting heavy weights and getting blisters and calluses. (Save any form of weights until several months after birth.) I love to feel sore muscles the next day and know that I really changed things up. But this kind of "whole hog" personality can get out of balance *really* quickly.

I found it hard to keep exercise training to the "little" corner of my life it merited. I believe in being active and living vigorously through the natural movement of a non-sedentary life, but it was the organized exercise sessions that I became obsessive about. If I didn't work out in the morning, it hung over my head like a *must* do all day. I couldn't relax!

Jeremiah 18:15 (NIV) says, "they burn incense to worthless idols, which made them stumble in their ways,." I had to lay down my idol and surprise, surprise . . . I have found better weight control and muscle definition by limiting myself to no more than four times a week. The much-needed healing rest and healthy hormone balance that I've gained from not overdoing it has given me a whole new lease on life. Now free from the obsession of "working out," I can see that it had become a false god in my life that sucked precious time, energy, and focus from things more important and eternal.

~Serene

"Body-Type-Ism"

What is the term used for looking down on a race? It's called racism. What is the term used for looking down on a gender? It's called sexism. What is the term used for looking down on a body type? Huh? I don't think there is one, so we'll we need to fix that. Here's a new "ism!" It's called body-type-ism! Anyone who looks down on a body type . . . is a *body-typist!*

Most of us won't end up looking "perfect." Each person is unique. Each one is beautiful, and God (the Creator) loves all body types, just like He loves men, women, and races of all kinds.

So should we.

~Meadow

thirteen

Prioritize

Recently I read this quote from St. Francis de Sales: "Every Christian needs a half an hour of prayer each day, except when he is busy, then he needs an hour." Immediately I was convicted and wrote beside it, "This is for me." My life is exceedingly busy each day (as I am sure yours is, too). It's easy to crowd out prayer when there is so much to do in our day and our list is so long. But what's the use of all our activities unless they are bathed in prayer? They are like hay and stubble, which will be burned up (1 Corinthians 3:12–15).

It's the same with reading the Bible. The more activities we pack into our lives, the less time we have to read God's Word. However, the busier we are, the more we need the sustenance of His Word. We'll soon get off the beaten track if we don't have daily doses to keep us in the right direction.

It affects our family life, too. When the schedule is full and everyone is going their various ways, it's easy for the family to become fragmented. Once again, the busier the family, the more we need to prioritize coming together as a family. Nothing is more important than gathering around the family meal table each day to connect, fellowship, pray, and worship together. Other things may seem necessary, but they are often detours from the enemy to keep us from God's best.

~Nancy

Learning Curve to Living Curve

Hebrews 12:1 says, "Let us run with patience the race that is set before us."

Serene: My seven-year-old just got a bike for his birthday. Even though he was excited for this present, he had a hard time enjoying it at first. He had not yet learned to ride a bike, so the first two weeks were more pain than pleasure. Through my kitchen window I watched him fall off so many times that I actually started feeling bad that we'd given him the bike. But he had a goal and he didn't give up. By the third week, he had surpassed mere riding. He was trick riding, standing on the bike seat with one leg in arabesque form, and raising one arm in victory! ❁

Some people open *Trim Healthy Mama* and want to find the place where we tell them exactly what to eat, in what portion sizes, and when. They don't want to think about it; they just want to be told what to do. But there is no such chapter because that is not really teaching somebody to ever ride by themselves. That would be just another cruel dead-end approach to dieting.

We explain that once they understand the life-changing principles in the book, they need to practice them in their own lives. This takes time; it takes falling off the bike, and it takes some bumps and bruises. But pretty soon you're riding, and before you know it, you're doing victory health laps and wowing yourself with accomplishments you never thought yourself capable of.

~Serene and Pearl

Emotional Eating

It's not just food that gives us unhappy feelings when we've gained too much weight. Oh, no! It's also food that gives us happy feelings! Or so we think. Fake hunger is often triggered by other Hs: Hatred, Hollowness—even Happiness.

It's when we get down on ourselves and we need some chocolate to lift ourselves up. We feel lonely and we comfort ourselves with a bag of chips. We have a reason to celebrate, so we reward ourselves with not one cookie but five!

This is the danger of emotional eating. But we can save ourselves when we realize the true cause of our hunger.

~Meadow

fourteen

Stamped with Royalty

My little four-year-old granddaughter, Breeze (Serene's daughter), has just run into my office dressed up as a princess, twirling around with happiness as she shows me her dress. In fact, all the little granddaughters love to dress up. They run to the dress-up box when they come to my home and never fail to dress up as princesses. It's inherently within them to do this. It's a God-given instinct.

Breeze loves to wear princess dresses every day of the year, even at home. One night at their dinner table, they were talking about marriage. Breeze's sister, Cherish, leaned over to Breeze and said, "Breeze, one day your prince is going to come to daddy and ask him for your hand in marriage."

Her eyes lit up with wonder, and then she looked down. "But I can't be wearing this dress," she exclaimed, and she began to describe the princess dress and jewelry she would wear and how she would do her hair!

As we get older, we succumb to the fashion of this world. We become victims of culture. However, no matter how we change our style, let's always remember that we are daughters of the "blessed and only Potentate, the King of kings, and Lord of lords" (1 Timothy 6:15). Because we are born in His image, we are stamped with royalty. We are representatives of a royal kingdom. Therefore, let's seek to speak, sit, walk, dress, and act like one who belongs to His holy, glorious, and royal kingdom.

~Nancy

Strengthen Yourself with Joy!

Nehemiah 8:10 says, "The joy of the Lord is your strength."

If we want to stay strong on our health journeys, we need to keep the joy around. This is not about enduring . . . but enjoying! It is important to laugh at yourself when you mess up, smile about the good things you get to eat, confess how blessed you are and how good you are feeling!

Decide to make this a happy journey. It won't be a perfect journey but you can spend it in joyous celebration rather than defeat. This joy will anchor you in strength and you won't be such easy prey to the wolves of doubt from your own mind or from others.

~Serene and Pearl

Milk or Meat

In 1 Corinthians 3:2, we read, "I have fed you with milk, and not with meat: for hitherto ye were not able to bear it, neither yet now are ye able."

A baby doesn't chew his food before he has his teeth
Nor can a newborn of the kingdom comprehend what is too deep
Milk is the ingredient to nourish a new life
The gospel is the milk, the gospel of the Christ
A baby will not grow without it; he will never learn to speak
And no one will make sense if they haven't had a drink
Like a baby at his birth, a Christian cries for life
For Christ himself came through birth, it was for life, He died
But this is not news to us if it was years ago
When we first tasted the milk, when we were just starting to grow
But did we grow? Did we ever reach the toddler stage?
Did we at least reach a point where we could waddle round and play?
Were we curious, adventurous, did we discover things?
We must have chewed on something because toddlers have their teeth
But were we useful? How did we share the milk if all we did was crawl?
An older child can pour a glass, if we reached that stage at all
Did our Father think us old enough to at least handle some chores?
If we were old enough, we wouldn't suck on milk bottles

Then what are we consuming? Surely something more
Surely all depends upon how much we have explored
What we explored in Scripture, by learning to perceive
What are we still living on? Is it the milk or is it the meat?
~*Meadow*

fifteen

Why Are We Scared?

Why are we so scared to trust God? Why are we so scared to trust Him with our lives when He is the God of the universe? Why do we think we can make better decisions than God when He is omniscient (all-wise and all-knowing)? I'm not condemning you; I'm guilty, too.

I wonder why many couples think that God could not provide for another baby in their family. Is it because we trust in ourselves rather than in our omnipotent (all-powerful) God?

Think about how many times have we prayed these lines in the Lord's Prayer: "Give us this day our daily bread" (Matthew 6:11). Do you notice that Jesus didn't teach us to pray, "Give us our monthly bread" or even our "weekly bread"? God wants us to learn to trust Him for *today*, knowing that He will be faithful again tomorrow.

God only sent enough manna for one day to the Israelites in the wilderness. If they couldn't trust God that He would provide for the next day and gathered extra just in case, it "bred worms, and stank" (Exodus 16:20)! That's what God thinks about our lack of trust in Him.

Let's pray with the hymn-writer, "Oh, for grace to trust Him more."

~Nancy

Pulling Down Strongholds

Sometimes, it's not simply a donut we are fighting against. The lure of destructive foods can be a powerful spiritual battle like the one we read in 2 Corinthians 10:4: "For the weapons of our warfare are not carnal but mighty through God for the pulling down of strongholds." Bringing our dietary weaknesses and food addictions before the One who is "mighty to save" is not a frivolous prayer topic.

Don't stamp failure on your journey because of emotional eating issues. The One who leads you in this has all the strength you need for the climb and the fight. He knows your struggles. He wants you to turn to Him for strength when the foods and habits that have enslaved you seem "stronger" than your own will power.

The weapons we fight with are God's; they are not weak. If we take hold of them, we can conquer.

~Serene and Pearl

Trusting Him

"There is no fear in love; but perfect love casteth out fear: because fear hath torment. He that feareth is not made perfect in love" (1 John 4:18). There is no fear in love, because love is also trust.

In a love story, two people come together who were both betrayed in the past. This gives them a reason to be reluctant to the idea of love. This gives them a reason to never trust again. But despite what could hold them back, they fall deeper into love than they ever had before. They trust *each other's* love. This is what God expects of us.

Everyone's been hurt. But every time God feels our pain, He is also hurt. He's been hurt more than anyone. He has been betrayed over and over again. But He will never betray us. His love comes with promises that we are to trust. And if we really love Him, we will also trust Him. That is faith.

~Meadow

sixteen

A New Vision

The table in your home is not only a place to eat some food and then run. It's a place to also feed the soul and spirit. It's a place for stimulating conversation and learning new things. It's a place to challenge our thinking.

In the Gospels we read that when Jesus came to a meal, He always taught something new. He exposed deceptions. He challenged thought patterns. He uncovered hypocrisy. (You can read some examples in Matthew 8:14–17; Luke 7:36–50; 11:37–54; 14:1–24; 14:15–24; 24:30–32; and John 21:9–19.)

Invite Jesus to your table. It will no longer be boring. Talk about life and what is happening in each other's lives. Ask questions. Bring subjects to the table to discuss—theological, spiritual, geographical, or political. At our table we laugh a lot. We discuss (and sometimes debate). We don't always agree, but this makes for stimulating conversation. My husband says, "We don't have to agree with one another, but we do have to love one another."

Ask God for a new vision for your table. Don't only think about what you will eat but also what you will talk about. Come prepared with a subject to discuss. Challenge each other's thinking. Invite Jesus to steer your conversation, teach you new things, and lead you in His truth.

~Nancy

Tasting His Goodness

Psalm 34:8 tells us "Oh taste and see that the Lord is good. Blessed is the man that trusteth in Him."

God has given us the gift of food as medicine. We can taste of his goodness daily! Yet many people are tasting only the perversion of foods, twisted and devitalized—hardly recognizable from their original form. This is not of the bounty of His goodness.

The above verse is first spiritual in meaning, but it does have a practical application. As Christians, we thank the Lord for our food and ask Him to bless the meal, but is sitting down to a fast-food burger, fries, and a soda really His food? The white, devitalized buns; the meat that may likely be only 50 percent meat and 50 percent who knows what; the potatoes fried in trans-fat vegetable oils; the soda that contains eight to ten teaspoons of sugar. Are these His gifts? If such a meal is all that is available, we believe He could supernaturally provide us with sustenance through these foods. But choosing these corrupted foods regularly is asking for a lot of miraculous power when He's already provided us with the good stuff.

The word "trusteth" in the last part of this verse is often translated as "take refuge in." While it is just as much of a pitfall to get caught in perfectionism when it comes to the purity of foods, you've also got to be sensible. And it doesn't make sense to allow our bodies to be constant receptacles for garbage. Only He knows the number of our days and food isn't everything. But let's keep the majority of our diet nutritionally rich and taste of His natural protection.

~Serene and Pearl

Called to Love

Suggested edit: In 1 John 4:20, we read: "If a man say, I love God, and hateth his brother, he is a liar: for he that loveth not his brother whom he hath seen, how can he love God whom he hath not seen?" The Greek word for "brother" translates both literally and figuratively. A brother (or sister) is someone who is a part of our lives. Maybe God put them there for a reason. This is why family and relationships are so important. Maybe this is also why Satan targets families. Siblings have quarreled since the beginning, much like they often do now. By keeping us from loving the Father, Satan tempts us to hate our brother.

What really hits me is the part in the verse where the brother is seen, but God is not. God is the most important one that we love. And He isn't seen. It should be easy to love someone who is seen, like our brothers and sisters. Yet many of us don't.

~Meadow

seventeen

Arise and Shine

Does your spirit cringe as you see evil encroaching more and more upon the land? My heart grieves, though God's Word tells us that "darkness shall cover the earth, and gross darkness the people." But my heart is also inspired by the rest of the prophecy: "Arise, shine; for thy light is come, and the glory of the Lord is risen upon thee . . . the Lord shall arise upon thee, and his glory shall be seen upon thee" (Isaiah 60:1, 2).

It's time for us to arise and shine. To eradicate all darkness and sin from our personal life and our home. A little glimmer of light is not enough to push back the darkness. We have to be a *great* light. Speaking of Jesus, Matthew 4:16 says, "The people which sat in darkness saw *great* light." What kind of light do people see in us? A faint glimmer? Or a great light? It won't just happen on its own. We have to *arise* and shine.

Let's remember that Jesus, the Great Light, dwells in our hearts and wants to shine His light through us. Let's make our marriage and our home a shining lighthouse, pointing the way to those who are groping in darkness. We know the Way, the Truth, and the Life. Why do we hide it? "Let your light so shine before men, that they may see your good works, and glorify your Father which is in Heaven" (Matthew 5:16).

~Nancy

Plant Your Roots in the Good Stuff

Psalm 1:3 says, "And he shall be like a tree planted by the rivers of water, that bringeth forth his fruit in his season; his leaf also shall not wither; and whatsoever he doeth shall prosper."

This picture is also painted again in Jeremiah 17. It describes this tree spreading her roots by the river. The tree's leaves stay green and the tree is not exhausted by the heat.

Of course, Christ is our living water, and He spiritually revives us so we never have to thirst again. But there is practical application, too. Jeremiah uses a physical picture to explain a spiritual truth. What river are your body's roots plugged into? Is it a river of soda, filled with chemicals, sugar, and bone-depleting phosphoric acid? Plug your roots into liquid that sustains life, and your body will bring forth fruit!

Lemon-Lime Trim Pop

Ingredients:
12 oz. pure sparkling water * Ice * Juice of ½ lemon and ½ lime (or use concentrate in the same amounts) * 2 doonks (which are 1/32 tsp. each) of THM Pure Stevia Extract Powder or 2 tsp. THM Sweet Blend (if you have an extra sweet tooth, try three of either).
Directions:
Squeeze lemon juice into large-sized jar.
Add THM sweetener and stir.
Add sparkling water and ice.
~Serene and Pearl

Life Decisions

My family loves to remind me how I was once a tantrum-throwing toddler. I was out of control, feisty, and fiery like my red hair, which made my mom want to tear out her hair. My poor mother would lie awake at night worrying about my outcome. Would I grow up to be a wild woman?

When I was six, I thought about my behavior as I watched my mom under stress from the back seat of the car. And I told her that I wanted to be good. She probably said something like, "That's good, Meadow," and thought, "Yeah, right."

But I really did want to be good.

After that moment, being bad was my dread. And if I ever was bad, it would plague me for a long time. I would even make confessions. Sometimes I tried to be so good that I'd say things like "Mom, I don't know if I lied, but what if it was a lie?" I was so scared of lying, and I valued my mom's instructions to act like a lady.

Of course, my decision to be good didn't mean I was suddenly perfect. But it greatly influenced my whole outlook on life. It goes to show you can make life decisions at any age, and you can stick to them.

~Meadow

eighteen

Extraordinariness!

Ordinariness. It's a place where many people live. I'm not talking about the "sameness" of your everyday tasks, for even the most mundane tasks are sacred, and therefore, extraordinary when you allow God into them. I am talking about living in the state of thinking like the status quo, fitting in with the humanist agenda of our society, and trusting in your own resources and understanding. There is no other word for this state than ordinariness.

To move out of this comfortable state and live with a biblical mindset takes you into extraordinariness. It is a challenging life—a realm of faith, hanging on the edge of a limb, adventures of trusting God when you cannot see where His provision is coming from, battles against the Adversary, speaking up for truth and God-given convictions in the face of popular opinion, and often receiving ridicule.

We are out of step with the world but in step with God. We are out of sync with public thinking, but we are listening to the mind of God. It's not the easy life, but it's definitely *not* ordinary.

Why live in ordinariness when you can live in extraordinariness? If God has anything to do with your life, it will be extraordinary, for God is never ordinary. Where do you and your family live?

~Nancy

Get Prepared

Proverbs 30:25 reminds us that "The ants are a people not strong, yet they prepare their meat in the summer." The Bible tells us in Proverbs several times to wisely consider the ways of the ants. Ants prepare!

One way that Serene and I are different is in how much food preparation we do. If this were a prepare-ahead contest, she would win hands down! But I do have a couple of easy, no-fuss food prep ideas that help streamline things.

Each week I bake up a three-pound bag of chicken tenderloins, then keep them in the fridge for easy protein access. (I start them frozen at 250 degrees for three hours so they are tender and easy to pull apart.) I use them all week, usually for quick lunches. I'll take out a couple tenderloins and sauté them in butter and seasonings for a Deep S salad or use them in a lighter salad in their leaner state. I can put them in Wonder Wraps (check out the recipe in *Trim Healthy Mama*). I'll make a chicken, cheese, and onion quesadilla for my husband with a couple of low-carb tortillas. I'll chop them up and add the pieces to soups for a protein boost. They help eliminate the "I'm stumped" feeling when I open the fridge.

I enjoy desserts, but I don't crave them the same way my husband does. His need for sweet treats is immense, and if I don't have desserts pre-made in the house, he'll forage for them on his own and end up at Baskin-Robins. So in the summer months, I make sure to always have a stock of Tummy Tucking ice cubes in my freezer. (Check out the recipe in *Trim Healthy Mama*.) I make a quadruple batch at a time, which gives my husband four days' worth of ice cream. He's one incredibly happy guy!

~*Pearl*

The Best Is Yet to Come

Over the decades, letters have evolved to telegrams to phones to cell phones to smart phones. The same goes with many other inventions. The funny thing is, we grow attached to each new invention, thinking that nothing could be better, until the next invention comes along, and then we think we can't live without that. We could never go back.

When we get too caught up in this world, we might believe that nothing could be better. But once we get to Heaven, we will see what we were missing out on. Nothing could be better. And we will never want to go back.

~*Meadow*

nineteen

Today's Thank You

God's purpose for our lives is to be "abounding with thanksgiving" (Colossians 2:7). That doesn't mean a "thank you" every now and then but a lifestyle abounding with thankfulness! Over the top with thankfulness! May we never be like the nine lepers, who after they were healed, went rejoicing on their way without ever bothering to thank the One who healed them (Luke 17:11–19).

What are you thankful for today?

T I am thankful for our family **Table** where we enjoy the presence of God, great laughs, family discussions, and where we make rich memories.

H I am thankful that God blessed me with my faithful **Husband** and that we have been married for nearly fifty-two years.

A I am thankful that God is **Always** available to hear my cry.

N I am thankful for my God-anointed career of **Nurturing** and **Nourishing** my family.

K I am thankful for God's **Kindness** and mercy to me.

F I am thankful for God's great **Faithfulness** to me, which is never failing.

U I am thankful for God giving me **Understanding** of His truth.

L I am thankful to God for **Loving** me enough to send His only Son to die for my sins and shed His precious blood.

~Nancy

Super Prepared Girl

You may not have strong will power or a penchant for healthy foods, but if you prepare for the cold blast of wintery temptations in the safety of summer weather, then you'll fare well. My nickname, coined by Pearl who is often bewildered at my fervor for preparing ahead, is "Super Prepared Girl." Here are some of my tips.

Unless it's a life-or-death mad rush out of the house, always throw a zippy or two of healthy munchies into your purse. A few zippy stuffer ideas could be a couple of squares of 85 percent dark chocolate and a handful of dry roasted almonds. Try a plan-approved protein bar and a cheese stick or two, or some celery stalks with unsweetened almond or peanut butter. Many times, I don't even need to eat these snacks, so I simply throw them back in the fridge as soon as I get home. But they are there to ensure I won't get HANGRY! (That's when you're so hungry that you get angry.) Oh, and pack them full enough to share if you are a social birdy.

If I am going out for an extended time and might miss a full meal, I always take my gorgeous little "Super Prepared Girl" cooler pouch with foods like an avocado-chicken-stuffed wonder wrap and my famous loaded Kefir smoothie in a clean salsa jar! Or I could pack an Ezekiel tuna wrap with loads of luscious lettuce and a light balsamic dressing in a tiny container. The options are endless.

If you don't have a little cooler, just throw a couple of handfuls of frozen berries in a jar with some plain Greek yogurt, a dash of THM Pure Stevia Extract, and a squirt of vanilla. The frozen berries keep the yogurt fresh, and by the time you are hungry, you will have a melted berry swirl of creamy wonderfulness!

~Serene

Get Up Again

"For all have sinned, and come short of the glory of God" (Romans 3:23). This is what every single one of us has in common—sin. The Greek meaning for "come short" also means to "fall short." We have all fallen out of God's glory. But the difference is that some of us decide to get back up . . . with help.

The following verse says, "Being justified freely by His grace through the redemption that is in Christ Jesus." Jesus holds out His hand to help us get up after a fall. It's our choice whether we want to take it or not. No one can be perfect, but everyone can make an effort.

~*Meadow*

twenty

Not Again!

It's time to cook supper. "Not again," you sigh. "Why can't I have a break from cooking night after night?" Preparing a meal for your family is not an insignificant undertaking. It's not a waste of time. It is very much a part of your mothering anointing. We see a beautiful depiction of a godly woman in 1 Timothy 5:10 (NASB), which gives a description of her "good works": "If she has brought up children, if she has shown hospitality to strangers, if she has washed the saints' feet, if she has assisted those in distress, and if she has devoted herself to every good work."

The word "brought up" is *teknotropheo* and means "to cherish, nourish, and give food to children." This is all about food! This means spending a lot of time in the kitchen! It's all part of the plan. And the bigger those children get, the more they want to eat.

Make every meal a "love affair." Don't do it with resignation but with revelation. You have the privilege of feeding your children nourishing food. You are gathering them together around your table again. You are also paving the way to feed them food that will nourish their soul and spirit. You are teaching them about life and passing on values to the next generation.

There is too much fast-food eating in our nation already! If you don't lovingly cook meals at home and pass on this tradition, what will the next generation do?

~Nancy

Narrow Expectations

If there is one lesson I have learned in my life that helps keep my joy around, it's this: I need to lay down my expectations. This has helped me immensely in my marriage of twenty years and in my health journey as well.

First Corinthians 13 tells us that love isn't self-seeking. That means when I show acts of love to my husband, I should not expect the same back. Don't get me wrong, I get plenty of love from my husband, but sometimes, it isn't shown in quite the way I I'm hoping. It's easy to miss the joy if I'm self-seeking and have narrow expectations.

Do I expect flowers? Perhaps I don't receive them but fail to notice he always puts gas in my car for me. If I choose to dwell on the lack of flowers, cards, poems, or letters (good grief, I spent *years* yearning for poems and letters), I completely miss the precious love he gives through multiple other measures.

What about your weight and health expectations? Are you so determined to lose one or two pounds every single week that you fail to notice that your nails and hair are healthier? Maybe you don't need to take that afternoon nap. Maybe you passed on the potato chips at a work function for the first time! Don't let expectations ruin the joy God wants you to experience.

~Pearl

Hard Work Won't Hurt Me

Today my muscles ache with a healthy pain from working out with some friends. Even though I am sore, I almost like the feeling. It tells me that I worked hard.

But what's even better than a physical healthy pain is often an emotional healthy pain. My mind might ache if I focus on something difficult for hours at a time. But when I finish, I'll know that I worked hard.

~Meadow

twenty-one

Hidden Glory

Great miracles don't always happen in the open. Jesus, the Son of the God of Glory, was conceived in the hidden place of the womb. This divine miracle happened in "the secret place," which is the term God uses for the womb (Psalm 139:15). The angel Gabriel told Mary that the Holy Ghost would come upon her and "thou shalt conceive in thy womb, and bring forth a son, and shalt call his name Jesus" (Luke 1:31). Although this conception was hidden, Jesus came forth to be revealed to the world as Savior and Deliverer.

It is similar with every conception. It doesn't take place in the open for everyone to see. God's handiwork (for only God gives conception) takes place in the recesses of the home and in the womb, the hidden part of the woman.

But this miracle doesn't stay hidden. Children are born who will one day come forth from the home to be the bearers of God's image on the earth.

In Psalm 128:3, God also gives the picture of the wife in the heart of the home (the Hebrew word means "the recesses, the inner part"). Is this because she is insignificant? No, it's because she is dwelling in her glory. God uses the same word "recesses" to describe the wife in the home as He does for the "inner sanctuary" of the temple where He dwelt in His Shekinah Glory (1 Kings 6:16).

From the recesses come forth great miracles and "sharpened and polished arrows" to change the world.

~Nancy

Keep on Asking

Matthew 7:7 says, "Ask, and it shall be given you; seek, and ye shall find; knock, and it shall be opened to you." God asks that we remind Him of His promises. His will is that we prosper and be in good health, but in my experience, His timing for answering our prayers rarely fits with our own time line.

When I married my husband, he was a road musician. All he had ever done was play music for a living. By the time we had two children, we both knew we did not want our children to grow up with their father gone for most of the year. He quit the road and got a job as a security officer at a nearby prison so he could help me with the children. The pay was terrible, the hours were long, and he had to work the overnight shift—a lot! That was seventeen years ago, and that was when I began praying for a *great* job for my husband, for blessing on his life, and that he'd be able to work in an area that he actually enjoyed. I don't think I ever missed a night praying this prayer over my husband and reminding God that my husband loved Him, served Him, and was an honorable man. Yet he only continued to find jobs that barely paid the bills. He didn't enjoy any of them but was thankful to have work.

Sixteen years of prayer later, God answered in a way far beyond what I could have hoped for. My husband and Serene's husband run the THM business now; they are home with us and incredibly busy but fulfilled!

Do not give up praying when circumstances look hopeless. Pray everything according to His will. Don't whine to God or demand your own will, but thank Him for His blessings and remind Him of His promises. Quote God's Word back to Him. He is our Father and only wants good things for us and for the ones we love! Sometimes those good things are in the form of a new job, financial peace, a restored marriage, or physical healing. Other times they are the growing of our faith when circumstances are bleak. Trust Him.

~*Pearl*

God's Kindness

I always delight in people's "Happy Birthday" wishes. But as I celebrated my my nineteenth, I wondered how much more amazing it would be to know that God was wishing me a "Happy Birthday" as well. He answered that thought with another one immediately: How blind of me! For if it is God who works in us to do good pleasure (Philippians 2:13), if good gifts only come from the Father (James 1:17), and therefore, kindness, then it was the Father who was kindly wishing me a Happy Birthday through others!

He told me "Happy Birthday" through personal greetings from family and friends, through phone calls, texts, messages, social media, and even through the warm smiles of random people I never met with before! He told me "Happy Birthday" too many times to count! He allowed me to feel blessed and encouraged with the uplifting words people poured into me. And as for the "happy" in my birthday, it was very happy indeed.

God is personal, even in little "Happy Birthday" wishes. And often the way God shows He is personal is through another person. Allow Him to use you.

~*Meadow*

twenty-two

Cement Your Convictions

Convictions don't come suddenly. They take time to reinforce. We often start off thinking this way or that, and we change our mind as we go along. We are influenced by society and what people around us think and say.

But we cannot stay "tossed to and fro, and carried about with every wind of doctrine." We must become cemented in our convictions. Ephesians 4:14 (NLT) says, "Then we will no longer be like children, forever changing our minds about what we believe because someone has told us something different or because someone has cleverly lied to us and made the lie sound like the truth."

Convictions become part of us as we seek after truth and search God's Word for understanding. Truth becomes "flesh and blood." When Jesus came, He was "made flesh . . . full of grace and truth" (John 1:14). The truth was part of Him. When truth is not only "a bit of head knowledge" but a part of who you are, you will not be intimidated by those who do not understand or even ridicule you for your stand. When truth is cemented in your heart, you will not change your mind even when you have opposition on all sides.

Godly convictions, rooted in God's Word, will stand up against all ridicule, debate, criticism, agnosticism, insurmountable difficulties, persecution, and "situational ethics."

~Nancy

Prepare-Ahead Day

Have a treat-making day where you stuff your freezer full of Skinny Chocolate, Coconut Divine Fudge Squares, Basic Treat Squares, Flax Seed Protein Bars, Easy Peazy Muffins, Just Like Wheat Thins, or whichever items you choose from the THM recipes. Take portions out of the freezer and put them into the fridge when you need to restore your edible stash. This way, you'll always have treats on hand.

It saves time to make double (or triple) batches of recipes so they are already prepared for future meals. Wonder Wraps (see *Trim Healthy Mama*) are a staple for my husband, and I always make double or quadruple batches! If I am making meatloaf, I make two and slice the other into lunchtime portions and freeze them in little baggies for a speedy lunch. Sunday night, when we all hang around talking, I flip a week's worth of Trim Healthy Pancakes while chatting with friends and family.

Be protein prepared. Pearl is a wise little ant when she makes her weekly chicken breasts for her fridge. I also like to keep a dozen hard-boiled eggs in the fridge for children's snacks or salad protein-boosters. I also like to buy no-drain pouches of salmon, tuna, or chicken to throw in my "Super Prepared Girl" bag or for easy at-home lunch preparation.

~Serene

It's More than Possible

Overcoming bad food habits is possible because we "can do all things through Christ who strengthens" us (Philippians 4:13). It's more than possible. It's not the biggest challenge when you really think about it. Christ Himself overcame the cross. Christ Himself said in John 16:33, "These things I have spoken unto you, that in me ye might have peace. In the world ye shall have tribulation: but be of good cheer; I have overcome the world."

What is food compared to a cross? What is food compared to the world? Bad food habits are only a minor *tribulation* compared to those. Don't let a little thing like being chained to food keep you from being of *good cheer*! If Christ overcame the cross, surely we can overcome bad food habits.

~Meadow

twenty-three

Where Are You Headed?

Because we live in the midst of a humanist society that rejects God and His infallible truths, we must constantly guard against being subtly assimilated into the culture. Even righteous people can be fooled.

Lot was a righteous man (2 Peter 2:7, 8) but the Bible says he "pitched his tent toward Sodom" (Genesis 13:12). He pointed the direction of his home toward this evil place when he could have pitched his home toward the mountains and been drawn toward God. What we look on, read, spend most of our time on, and think about is what we will become. Soon, Lot and his family ended up living in Sodom (Genesis 14:12). Then we read of how he became totally entrenched in the city life. He even became an elder in the Gate of Sodom (Genesis 19:1).

He was still a righteous man who trusted in God, but he lost most of his family! When he tried to warn his sons-in-law, sons, and daughters to run from the coming judgment, they thought he was crazy. They were entrenched in the culture—and were destroyed (Genesis 19:12–28).

What is the passion and direction of your family? The direction you are pointed is where you will end. Keep pointed toward God's ways.

~Nancy

Weighed in the Balances

As we watched a dramatized portrayal of the book of Daniel one family movie night, we saw the severed hand write on the plaster of the king's palace. My children were pretty thrilled with the special effects. But I knew the story so well from my childhood, I wasn't in as much shock and awe.

I went to the restroom in the middle of the night, and the words "MENE, MENE, TEKEL, UPHARSIN," whammed into my heart! Deep inside my soul, I felt the burning question, "You have been weighed in the balances. Have you been found wanting?"

King Belshazzar was found wanting. God numbered his kingdom and finished it. He didn't glorify God who held his breath in His hands.

What kingdom do I spend my time serving? Belshazzar lifted himself up against the Lord of Heaven. Have I been lifting up my own dreams and plans—my "to-do" lists, priorities, and comforts—above God's purpose for giving me breath? Am I spending too much of my time focusing on earthly things that vie for my heart?

Will I be found wanting today? Will I be alive to the kingdom of God and His design for me? Will my husband and children know they are my true treasures?

~Serene

Let's Raise the Standard

People make up stereotypes for every stage in life. For that reason, that's who they are expected to be—and often the way they act. People say, "They're just teenagers, they shouldn't have to worry about anything right now. Let them have fun while they're still young." And because the low standards for youth are a general idea, it's become acceptable.

But consider 1 Timothy 4:12: "Let no man despise thy youth; but be thou an example of the believers, in word, in conversation, in charity, in spirit, in faith, in purity." If we were to be what society generally expects us to be, we would be lazy yet irrational, independent yet demanding, and disrespectful yet wanna-be-respected youth! These are all reasons why youths could be despised! However, if we are to be the examples God wants us to be, we will be enthusiastically hardworking at our tasks, joyfully giving, eager to listen, slow to speak, pure in a polluted world, and prove that time is not the reason for behavior. Choice is.

Any youth who holds these qualities is in a position to be admired instead of despised.

~Meadow

twenty-four

Inside and Out

Yesterday we talked about Lot, who lost most of his family. Noah also lived in a culture of evil, filth, and violence. He didn't have one other person standing with him. His children had no righteous friends. Everyone around them was corrupt! But he saved his family. How did he do it?

He built an ARK. He built an **A**nointed haven to protect his family from the storms of life. He built a **R**ock of truth against the deceptions of society. And he built a little **k**ingdom of Heaven on earth. He built it according to God's specifications, not his own ideas (Genesis 6:22). He secured it "within and without with pitch" (Genesis 6:14). He made sure that it was not only watertight on the outside but also on the inside, too.

It is not enough to protect our children from the storms raging outside our home. We must watch that we don't have storms going on inside the home. In-house storms often do more damage than outside storms!

May God anoint you with His wisdom and strength to seal your home inside and out.

~Nancy

Don't Bring the Bread

Recently we went out to dinner with our parents and husbands. We ordered wonderful meals—steaks with sides of salad and asparagus for our husbands, while we looked forward to grilled salmon with creamed spinach. We were having a blast with funny dinner discussion when the waiter suddenly appeared with three baskets of dinner rolls. We'd forgotten to say, "Don't bring the bread."

Pearl: *"We hadn't missed bread until it sat in front of our noses, steaming white yeast rolls begging to be buttered and wolfed down! Healthy hunger turned into desperate cravings—the temptation was too much. We fell like dominoes starting with my husband, Charlie. Sam (Serene's husband) soon followed suit. I tried hard to hold out as our dad joined the men buttering up some of that bread, but I have to admit, I couldn't make it—even with a strong lecture from Serene. That girl never cheats!* ❖

The Bible tells us to run away from temptation. God knows we are too weak when something tempting is dangled right before our eyes. Plan A is to opt out of temptation by asking the waiter to hold the bread or not to bring the dessert menu (super special occasions don't apply). If the situation is complicated (dinner with coworkers or with husbands who are not inclined to give up dinner rolls) try plan B: throw a delicious snack into a zippy and carry it in your purse to the restaurant to nibble on while your food is being prepared.

~Serene and Pearl

A Child of God

"When I was a child, I thought as a child: but when I became a man, I put away childish things. For now we see through a glass, darkly; but then face to face: now I know in part; but then shall I know even as also I am known" (1 Corinthians 13:11, 12).

These verses warn me, comfort me, and delight me. But they also intrigue me.

I am more in the dark than I realize, even as a Christian. By putting away my childish thoughts, I am humbled to see that I really am like a child. And the more I come to know, the more I realize that I barely know anything at all.

~Meadow

twenty-five

Handicapped or Free?

Are you weighed down by a heavy burden today? Maybe you are facing a huge trauma. Or perhaps it is the accumulation of many little worries and problems that add up to a big weight. Are you going to keep carrying this load around? It makes you so tired. You can hardly get through the day. You can't live life effectively when you are weighed down. You can't even mother efficiently. You are handicapped. God knows this, and therefore tells us to "lay aside every weight, and the sin which doth so easily beset us" (Hebrews 12:1).

Do you notice that this Scripture tells us to lay it aside? It actually means "to strip it off." Take some action. Come to Jesus. Come to the foot of the cross and throw down your burden. Don't hang on to it. Sometimes we are tempted to hang on to it so we have something to groan and complain about. What a delusion!

Let it go and look to Jesus. He showed us the way. He endured the cross and the shame because of the joy set before Him. When you take your eyes off the burden and lift your eyes to Him, He will give you new perspective and show you His eternal plan.

Now you can run your race. Now you'll have energy! Now you can keep going to the finishing line.

~Nancy

Hear His Kindness

Sometimes our trials are consequences from our own sins and a loving punishment from God who wants to steer us back on track. Other times they are training us for growth and honing our character. It is God's great kindness and love that draws us to travel through these deep valleys so we can experience His comfort. It is in the depths that He births a new maturity in us.

My name Serene means peace and tranquility, but this is where my greatest battle was fought. I have always loved Jesus, but I also struggled with a pit of fear that shackled my soul. God ordained circumstances where my husband had to work overseas in the Middle East and out of state for a couple of years to make ends meet. I couldn't rely on my husband to feel safe when the wind creaked the house at night or when my little ones were sick. I had to find my deep anchor in my loving Father.

Night after night, I went to sleep whispering over and over the name of Jesus. I imagined my family nestled safely in His hand where nothing but the storms of His perfect will could blow. And I found Him—more gentle, more tangible, and more intimately than I ever knew Him before. He spoke words of kindness in my loneliness. I ran into His embrace and found my rest.

God says in Hosea 2:14 (NASB): "Therefore, behold, I will allure her, bring her into the wilderness, and speak kindly to her." The Hebrew word *lev* for "kindly" means "from my heart and soul, a deep heart to heart talk." I cherish the words He buried deep into my soul, "I am your Haven of rest."

~Serene

His Love Is Stronger

If feelings are made in the image of our Father in Heaven, then our love is just an idea of His love. If our pain is a consequence of that love, then our pain is just a taste of His pain—pain which He must endure every second of every day that is more excruciating than we could ever imagine. It's pain that He does not deserve, but sometimes, we deserve.

No one wants to bear the feeling of loss when the ones we know the best, the ones we love the most, leave us. If everyone realized that God's feelings are stronger, that He knows us better than we know ourselves, that He loves us more than anyone ever could, that He was there all along—would we still leave Him?

~Meadow

twenty-six

Conformed or Transformed?

You have probably memorized Romans 12:2: "Be not conformed to this world: but be ye transformed by the renewing of your mind, that ye may prove what is that good, and acceptable, and perfect, will of God." The word "transformed" is *metamorphoo* in Greek. Because we understand the metamorphosis of a caterpillar changing into something completely different, we get to see the full understanding of this word.

We are not to change slightly from the culture of this society. Through the constant filling of the Word of God and the Holy Spirit in our lives, we are to change into completely different people. We are to live a totally different lifestyle than the humanistic society around us.

Metamorphoo is the same word that is used when Jesus was "transfigured" in front of Peter, James, and John. He didn't slightly change; He was totally transformed. "His face did shine as the sun, and his raiment was white as the light" (Matthew 17:1, 2).

The J. B. Phillips translation says, "Don't let the world around you squeeze you into its own mold." Williams' translates it, "Stop living in accordance with the customs of this world." If we are living pretty much like everyone in society around us, we are most probably entrenched in the humanistic culture and don't even know it! God wants to transform us into a totally different person, one that lines up with His biblical culture.

We are either conformed or transformed. Which one are you?

~Nancy

Will You Let Go?

I suffered with fear as a little girl, but it became worse when I grew up and had children. I worried about their safety and all the "what ifs" that could happen to them. My heart pounded in my chest if I lost sight of one of my toddlers. I had CPR tips taped all over my fridge. Even though this is a good idea for committing these safety tips to memory, I knew I was controlled by this fear.

As a family, we also went through a season of extreme stress and my adrenals were not strong enough to weather it. I ended up suffering with major panic attacks before I let go and let God hold me the way He always wanted to. He longed to be my haven where I could rest in His arms, but I perched stiffly on the end of His lap grasping on to my "what ifs" like a poisonous toy.

Are you tired of clinging onto fear but have held it for so long that you don't know how to let go? Cry out to your Daddy. He is closer than you think and hears the faintest cry. Psalm 29:11 says, "The Lord will give strength unto his people; The Lord will bless his people with peace."

Are you ready to receive His rest?

~Serene

A Little More Effort

Many people worry about failing. That's because they don't want to try. You don't only fail from trying. Most of the time, you fail from not trying.

For those people who skip the THM plan because they don't think they'll get anywhere, they're not getting anywhere anyway. It can only get better with a little effort.

~Meadow

········· twenty-seven ·········

Your Lowest Point

Are you at a low pit in your life? Do you feel you are in a dark dungeon? Please don't despair! Even if you're in the lowest pit, God has not forgotten you.

Jeremiah was in a literal dungeon, sinking in the mire. His captors didn't want him to live. But there is no low place too low for God to come. Cry out to the Lord as Jeremiah did, "Waters flowed over my head; I said, 'I am cut off!' I called on Your name, O Lord, out of the lowest pit. You have heard my voice, 'Do not hide Your ear from my prayer for relief, from my cry for help.' You drew near when I called on You; You said, 'do not fear'" (Lamentations 3:54–57 NASB).

Don't look around at the dark dungeon that seems to envelop you. Look up to the Lord, and cry out to Him. When you turn your eyes to Him, He will draw near to you. He whispers to you, "Do not fear." In fact, He has a "Do not fear" promise for every day of the year in His Word. He reminds you, "I will never leave you or forsake you" (Hebrews 13:5, 6). He is with you even when you cannot feel His presence. Trust Him.

~Nancy

Haven Rest

My youngest child is now two years old. Her name is Haven Rest, a name that symbolized the soul rest God was birthing in me. I had finally come to the deep place of refuge God had for me. I had quieted my soul in Him and come home to my haven, His bosom. I had spent my whole life craving this haven but had to give up my fears to enter in. Fear had become so familiar to me that I didn't realize how much I served it.

Minutes after the birth of my little baby Haven Rest, God tested the spiritual birth of my willingness to rest in Him. Her chest heaved and her nostrils flared as she struggled for each breath. As she was rushed into an oxygen tent and hooked up to monitors, the stormy waves of her breathing were charted. For a week, the doctors poked and prodded and went through the gamut of tests, all to find no reason for her distress other than the guess that she had swallowed fluid during her birth.

I was far from home with encouragement from family as we were living in the town of my husband's temporary job for my final trimester. My husband worked twelve hours, seven nights a week, and was asleep when I longed to pick up the phone and cry to him. I needed God to speak to me, and he did beyond my wildest expectations.

God's words are true: "In the day of my trouble I will call upon thee: for thou wilt answer me" (Psalm 86:7).

~Serene

Finding the Balance

I am seeking to find a balance between understressed and overstressed. When I am too relaxed, I feel lazy and useless. When I am overstressed, I feel anxious and depressed. They key is to find that balance in between. Yet again, I bring up Romans 5:3 about how we are to "rejoice in our sufferings." A little stress is good. It trains the character and keeps our lives driven and exciting.

As I casually make it through another day, I know that I can make time to enjoy the simple things—go on walks, strum my guitar, catch up with friends, and sip my tea. But I also know that I must make time for the important things—cleaning, working, studying, and reading my Bible. I want to be at peace as I seek to make a change.

~Meadow

twenty-eight

The Best Entertainment

My youngest daughter, Mercy, spent the day with Serene and the children. At the dinner table, she shared how it was such a *fun* day. "It was a laugh a minute," she said, "With all their funny antics and the things they say, children are the *best* entertainment."

Isn't it so true? How sad that many miss out on so much joy because they don't want children. They have been robbed by a society that conditions them to think that children are too much work and are a hindrance to their plans. But sadly, they miss out on experiencing the joys and blessings of children.

God equates mothering and children with joy. In Psalm 113:9 it says, "He maketh the barren woman to keep house, and to be a joyful mother of children. Praise ye the Lord." Notice that this Scripture about joyful mothering ends with praising the Lord! Not with being miserable and unhappy.

Here's just one of the conversations Mercy shared with us from that day:

> *Shepherd*: "I don't want to be a girl."
> *Serene*: "Why?"
> *Shepherd*: "Because girls lay babies."

I think they must have too many chickens around their house!
~Nancy

My Desired Haven

While in the hospital with Haven, I remembered a tattered little New

Testament in my purse. I had meant to throw it away many times, as it had so many missing pages. It belonged to my mother when she was a teenager, and I don't even know how it ended up in my purse!

I grabbed it in my moment of desperation and pleaded with God for a personal word. I opened it and my eyes immediately fell on an underlined section. Before I got too excited, I flipped through the rest of the Bible to see if there were any other underlined passages. None! Could this be a special word for me?

I read Psalms 107:27–31: "They cry unto the Lord in their trouble, and he bringeth them out of their distresses. He maketh the storm a calm so that the waves thereof are still." I thought of the stormy waves on Haven's monitor. The nurse said that when the waves settled down, I could take her home! "Then are they glad because they be quiet; so he bringeth them unto their desired haven." Did I read that correctly? My "desired *Haven*." It was all my heart ached for!

I didn't know the word "haven" was in the Bible. In fact, that verse is the only place it appears in the Bible. My mother had underlined this passage when she was a young teenager in New Zealand, and God used it many decades later to speak peace to my soul in Mississippi, USA, and bring hope for her thirty-seventh grandchild. "Oh that men would praise the Lord for his goodness, and for his wonderful works to the children of men!"

~Serene

Pep Talks

For those of us who are thinkers, it's easy to get carried away as we lie in our beds at night. We wonder if we're doing anything right with our life. We give ourselves pep talks to do better, and we make late-night life decisions.

When the morning comes with the regular routine, we forget about our concerns and carry on as if it were any other day.

Then the night comes. We decide to do better. Then the morning comes, and it's another regular day.

How do we break this pointless cycle? By giving ourselves pep talks during the day, at the very moment when the temptation hits us.

~Meadow

twenty-nine

Where Do Tables Originate?

What kind of table do you have in your home? Round or rectangular? Old and shaky? Shiny and brand new? It really doesn't matter what it looks like, but the important thing is what happens around your table. Your table is the most central piece of furniture in your home.

Did you know that God loves tables? And do you know where they originated? Did you know they go back even further than the Bible? Yes, they originated in Heaven! They are God's idea. God has a table in His heavenly kingdom. When Jesus spoke to His disciples of His home in Heaven, He promised them that one day they would "eat and drink at my table in my kingdom" (Luke 22:30). Check out Matthew 8:11 and Luke 13:29, too.

God's picture of a family focuses on them sitting around the table. I like the Living Bible translation of Psalm 128:3: "Your wife shall be contented in your home. And look at all those children! There they sit around the dinner table as vigorous and healthy as young olive trees." Where are the children? Not sitting in front of the TV. Not eating on the run. They are all together around the table. And the next verse says, "Behold, thus shall the man be blessed that feareth the Lord."

It's a picture of the heavenly kingdom. Why not make our homes a taste of Heaven on earth now?

~Nancy

Tight Budget or Perfect Provision?

"I don't have the budget to eat healthy." Have you heard this from others before, or are you one who says it? The truth of the matter is that healthy, slimming food can be friendly to your pocketbook.

You don't have to buy your food from a fancy health-food supermarket to find your trim figure or gain vitality. In fact, these stores are often traps for gimmicks and packaging. An organic, gluten free, non-GMO box of macaroni and cheese packed in a box made from recycled material, printed with soy ink, trade free, and rain forest compliant (that costs two bucks more) has no different impact upon your blood sugar than the eighty count box of mac-n-cheese from a budget grocer. They're both destructive to your health.

Maybe you cannot afford all organic; maybe you can only afford the ground beef on sale with coupons at a dollar store. There are tens of thousands of women on the THM plan who have beaten debilitating medical issues and have found their waistline with nothing fancier.

God is our provider and wants you to be in good health. If your budget is tight, this does not mean God removes His blessings from the sensible foods you can actually afford.

~Serene and Pearl

Content

"Not that I speak in respect of want: for I have learned, in whatsoever state I am, therewith to be content" (Philippians 4:11).

When I wrote the song "Almost Eighteen," I counted my years from one to seventeen, and told how I was looking forward to eighteen. I wasn't telling my life story but expressing my mixed feelings. I missed being a carefree little girl who could be content with playing outside all day. And then I looked back on my early teen years, when I was often anxious. What freedom and joy I've found since then!

Stepping into the adult world caused me to be both nervous and excited, all at the same time. It was as if I had been on a very long and full journey, and I was about to start an even longer and fuller journey.

It was my hook "Now I'm just embracing almost eighteen" that made it clear how I really felt. I was happy with the state I was in, embracing both the past and the future. They came together to create a perfect balance in the present. And now that I'm eighteen, I like where I'm at now.

~Meadow

thirty

Homeness

It's a rainy day here in Tennessee but still beautiful as the fresh, green leaves begin to fill the trees after the barrenness of winter. And it's cozy inside our home. It's our sanctuary. Our place of rest.

I recently read the word "homeness" in one of George McDonald's books. I like this word, don't you? I'm going to add it to my vocabulary. It conjures up so many loving and warm thoughts and memories.

I was reading in Ezekiel 34 (Knox translation) about Israel coming back to their homeland. It gives such an understanding of how God feels about our homes. He says, "They shall have pasture on the hill-sides of Israel, by its watercourses, in the resting-places of their home . . . with soft grass for them to rest on, rich feed for them to graze. Food and rest, says the Lord God, both these I will give to my flock . . . a blessed people in a blessed home."

God wants our home to be a place where He can rest and where we can rest as a family. Of course, that doesn't mean to say we are not all working hard, but we do it in an atmosphere of rest, not tension and strife. Let's deal severely with anything that disturbs our "resting place." Proverbs 24:15 says, "Lay not wait, O wicked man, against the dwelling of the righteous; spoil not his resting place."

Make "homeness" the rich ambiance of your home.

~Nancy

Women and Muffins

There is absolutely no Scripture we can find to support a reason for including this topic in a devotional, but we know that we as women are devoted to muffins; the connection goes deep and should never be severed. We know that eating an ooey-gooey, chocolatey muffin makes us nicer people, and God wants us to be kind. We also know that you want to get rid of your muffin top, and what better way to do it than by eating muffins!

This afternoon, sit down for a few minutes, and enjoy this muffin with a cup of coffee for your health and sanity. (And to make this a spiritual occasion, keep your Bible near to snatch a few verses during the calm.)

Volcano Mud Slide Muffin

Ingredients:

1 egg * 2 flat Tbs. Golden Flax Meal * 2 rounded Tbs. unsweetened cocoa powder * 3 tsp. THM Sweet Blend * ½ tsp. aluminum-free baking powder * 1 flat Tbs. coconut oil or butter * choice of 1 Tbs. water or ¼ cup berries (raspberries or chopped strawberries)

Instructions:

Crack egg into coffee cup or oven-safe ramekin and whisk well with a fork.

Add all other ingredients except berries, and mix very well with a fork. If adding berries, stir gently into batter at the end.

For microwave version, cook on high for only 40 seconds if using only water. If including berries, it will need to be closer to a minute. The muffin should be gooey in the center when you take it out.

Oven versions should take between 8-12 minutes at 350F. Take out of oven before top of muffin is completely set.

Top with Greek yogurt or a swirl of heavy cream.

~Serene and Pearl

Enjoy the Now

We're humans. By nature, we are never satisfied. We are always looking for the next thing to do, the next thing to take, the next thing to entertain us, and the next foods we're going to indulge in.

Sometimes I try to fight this feeling of unsatisfaction. When I take in my surroundings and think about the now, I am content.

~Meadow

thirty-one

Wombness

Yesterday we talked about "homeness." I'm going to stretch your vocabulary a little further and introduce "wombness." Wombness is not some ethereal imaginative word. It is a reality! It is very much part of who we are as women. In fact, you would not be a woman if you did not have a womb! It also reveals a beautiful character of God. The womb is more than a place where a baby is conceived and grows. It is the seat of our yearning and compassion.

The Hebrew word *racham* is used to describe the literal womb of a woman, but this same Hebrew word is also used to describe God. It reveals God's compassion and tender mercy. It is translated "compassion" four times, and "mercy" thirty times. When we embrace our wombness, we reveal the compassion of God.

The meaning of "feminine" in the 1828 Webster's Dictionary is as follows: "The first syllable is probably from *womb* . . . The last part of the word is probably from man, quasi, *femman*, womb-man. To be feminine is to be 'a womb man.'"

Don't despise your wombness. It is a very integral and beautiful part of who you as a woman.

~Nancy

Don't Stay in the Brambles

Psalm 119:176 says, "I have gone away like a lost sheep." God called David a man after his own heart, yet even David found himself led astray. We all veer off course. We stumble, fall, and let ourselves down. Yet the Good

Shepherd never leaves us alone. He leaves the ninety-nine sheep that are safe and sound to rescue the one stuck in the thorns.

Do you feel off course today? Did you get tangled up in a bag of thorny potato chips last night? Did you get stuck in the briar patch of Breyers ice cream? Hold on a minute. We're relating potato chips and ice cream to spiritual themes? Yes. Does God care if we eat potato chips? Probably not. But He does care if we are stuck in a cycle of guilt, shame, and unhealthy habits which are the cause of these feelings.

You don't have to stay stuck in the brambles. He wants you released. Don't stay in condemnation just because you messed up. Let His crook untangle you from the thorns, and let Him carry you to healthier pastures today.

~Serene and Pearl

Let the Spirit Win

"So letting your sinful nature control your mind leads to death. But letting the Spirit control your mind leads to life and peace" (Romans 8:6). Our sinful nature comes from the flesh. Our bodies are made of flesh. The flesh will never be satisfied. It constantly demands. Craves. It doesn't want to do labor by working out and getting into shape! It only wants to be served. It will always want more, more, and more food. Especially the food it shouldn't have.

This might keep the body pleased, but eventually, it could lead to an early *death*. Our spirit, however, is always at war with the body. The spirit is in distress when the body is the dictator, thus, stealing away the *life* and *peace*.

Let the spirit win. Take control of your flesh today.

~Meadow

thirty-two

Scare the Devil

The ark kept Noah and his family safe from the flood. But although they were safe, they had to go through the storm. We will never be able to avoid the storms and tempests of this life. Consequently, we must learn how to navigate them. God shows the way through the example of Noah who built a strong home, a home that could withstand the biggest tempest that ever hit this earth.

Each one of us faces our different storms. We may face even bigger storms ahead. The most important thing we can do is to continue to strengthen our inner man, our marriage, and our home. Ask God to show you any leaks where the destroying enemy can enter. Our home constantly needs repair. I am glad I married a "Mr. Fix-it" (as I call my husband). However, even more damaging than physical wear and tear is spiritual wear and tear.

Constantly check what is going on in your home. What are your children watching on the electronics in your home? The enemy hates godly homes and he looks for openings in the walls where he can enter in.

Close up all the holes. Take authority over compromise, worldliness, and all evil. Plead for God's protection. Cover your home with the precious blood of Jesus Christ. Become such a diligent watchwoman that you scare the devil!

~Nancy

Sip All Day, Don't Snack All Day

Constantly pecking at food when your digestive system was designed to have rest periods upsets the sensible rhythm of your digestion. This is like constantly adding to the washing machine when it is mid-cycle. However, keeping yourself hydrated with yummy thirst quenchers is a way of warding off needless nibbling and can help you break any soda addiction.

Snacks are important but often our *mouth* just wants something. This is not true hunger. It's a desire for hand-to-mouth satisfaction like a baby who wants a pacifier. Support yourself emotionally and physically with one of our All Day Sippers. Not only do these drinks hydrate your body and ward off tired slumps, they treat you with happy bursts of taste sensation and contain medicinal ingredients to heal your body.

You've probably never heard anyone suggesting you drink moonshine in a devotional before, but try our Good Girl Moonshine recipe. We call this a Baptist-friendly buzz toddy. There's no alcohol, but it does make you say "EeeeeAhhhh!" as it goes down your throat. It is zingy, zippy, revitalizing, and the ginger and apple cider vinegar rev your metabolism and fight inflammation.

We promise it is perfectly legal.

Good Girl Moonshine

Ingredients:

1 tsp. ginger powder * 2–3 Tbs. apple cider vinegar (purchase the one with the "mother) * Pure THM Extract Powder to taste (2–3 doonks, which are 1/32 tsp. each) * water or sparkling water, ice * optional extracts like lemon, caramel, orange, or coconut, or add therapeutic essential oils to taste.

Directions:

Fill a quart jar with ice, add all ingredients, fill to the top with water, and stir well. Sip all day!

~Serene and Pearl

To Self-Indulge or Not

I would really enjoy a movie right now. Monday's just around the corner, and I have the right to make the most of these last few hours of my weekend! I have the freedom to relax and to be entertained . . . to please myself.

But I know what will happen. While I am *enjoying* myself, I will also be *lecturing* myself. "It would be better if I was writing right now." Or "What if I was praying and reading my Bible instead?"

So instead of watching a movie, I am writing. Plus, I have another plan. I know that pleasing God will not only satisfy Him, but it will also satisfy me more than just seeking to please me.

I'm not against movies. I love to watch movies with friends, families, and as an occasional "just me" treat. But resting doesn't always mean *self-indulging*.

~Meadow

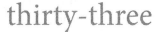

thirty-three

Two Special Times

We make two special times each day to take time out from our busy lives to come into the presence of the Lord, to listen to His Word, and speak to Him. These times are our morning and evening Family Devotions. It seems to me that it is the very least we can give to God in our daily family life.

When we each have a turn to pray, I am so glad for the opportunity to thank God again, out loud, for His great salvation—and that Jesus was willing to take upon Himself my sin and the sin of the world. I don't think that we will ever, with our finite minds, be able to comprehend the enormity of the great salvation that has been given to us. Even our morning and evening devotions each day are not enough to thank Him. It will take all eternity to give honor to the Lamb who was slain from the foundation of the world.

May our lives be worthy of His dying for us. To have this in our heads throughout the day will make a difference to us personally and to how we live and act.

Make sure you have your two special times each day in your family, too.

~Nancy

Companion of Fools

"He that walks with wise men shall be wise, but a companion of fools will be destroyed" (Proverbs 13:20).

We had a neighbor who became a great friend of ours. She was in her early twenties and was naturally inclined to healthy foods. She never struggled with her weight until she took a new job. In less than a year she'd put on close to forty pounds and came to us, distraught.

The gals at her work were always on some sort of diet but would binge on donuts in the afternoon after the "diet shake" lunches or calorie-restricted breakfasts. She found herself commiserating with her friends and joining in with the donut pity parties. Her new sugar addiction went beyond the donut splurges at work—she'd started to binge on sugar in the evenings, too.

We encouraged her with many ideas for healthy, sweet treats she could take to work or eat in the evening. But in the end, if that job and the influence of her coworkers were going to be the undoing of her health, an hourly rate was not worth it!

We are not advising anyone cut off relationships over food, but if Friday nights with the girls at Dairy Queen are your undoing for the rest of the week, then design other times to get together with those friends that don't center around destructive food events. Get proactive about changing the scenery.

~Serene and Pearl

I Do It for Him

I shouldn't worry about my health. I shouldn't work out in order to feel more empowered than others. I shouldn't wish to look my best for my own vanity. I shouldn't spend hours surfing Google about health and fitness just for my information alone.

I do all of that—but I don't want to do it just for me.

My body is made of dust, and someday it will return to dust. We're all going to die eventually. Why should I obsess about something that's only temporary? There are people who are under the rule of their own bodies. I want to help free them.

Someday, I may no longer be a single girl looking out for myself and will have my own family. My family will depend on my health.

Although I am just dust, this dust has miraculously been made into a temple. And I will polish it until it shines if it is able. I will clean it up and take care of it so that it can function.

This temple is not my own—though the upkeep is my responsibility. I don't just do it for me—I do it for those who depend on me and I do it for Him.

~Meadow

thirty-four

Oh, the Wonder

What a beautiful sight as I beheld all Serene's children gather around their new baby sister, Haven Rest. And not only her children but also all the cousins, too. They each wanted a turn to hold the baby, some getting upset because they hadn't yet had a turn. Their eyes were filled with wonder and delight. The room was suffocating with children, and Serene had to steal her precious baby away to feed her.

Oh, the joy of new life. There is no greater wonder and blessing that can come into the home than a new precious life that comes freshly from the hand of God, "the descent from Heaven of a new soul," a child destined by God for specific purposes on this earth and who will live forever.

There is no greater gift to give children; there is nothing they would rather have than another baby sister or brother. And no matter how many children in the family, the wonder and excitement never fades.

This is the "life" of family. How sad that modern Christianity has been seduced by the enemy who hates life to limit their families. They not only limit children but also dynasties to come. They also miss out on the joy, laughter, wonder, delight, and the divine visitation that comes with a new life from God.

~Nancy

Your Posture Speaks

Psalm 20:8 says, "They are brought down and fallen: but we are risen and stand up right."

Does your posture speak of defeat or of the victory to be found in

Christ? Not only does a slouch tell others that you are downtrodden, it sends chemical messages to your own mind and body. A stance that looks strong and happy releases positive neurochemicals, but a droopy posture makes you feel emotionally droopy.

Make your posture smile! We don't mean push your shoulders back so much that you look uncomfortable and stiff. All you have to do is stand tall and elongate the back of your neck. Think of a string gently pulling the back of your head higher and happier. This will tuck your stomach in, pull your shoulders back, and naturally align your spine. Stand confidently as a beautiful creation of God.

~Serene and Pearl

I'm Humbled

Everyone has had pride at least once in their life, if not regularly. But maybe not everyone is aware of it. Those who believe they've never had pride are probably prideful about that very fact alone.

How do we maintain a humble state? I find that by simply being aware of the shameful fact that I'm prideful, I am humbled.

~Meadow

thirty-five

Beware

No, I am not trying to scare you. I'm just reminding you of 2 Peter 3:17 where it exhorts us to "beware lest ye also, being led away with the error of the wicked, fall from your own steadfastness." We cannot afford to be status quo. We cannot afford to be average. We cannot afford to be mediocre. This Scripture reminds us that even those who are steadfast in the faith can fall if they are not purposefully pressing on. The word "fall" also means "to be driven off one's course." 1 Corinthians 10:12 says, "Wherefore let him that thinks he stands take heed lest he fall."

How do we keep on course? The next verse in 2 Peter 3:18 tells us "But grow in grace and in the knowledge of our Lord and Savior Jesus Christ." We must keep growing—increasing and enlarging in our faith and walk with God. If we are not growing, we are in danger of falling.

We must guard against deception. We cannot imbibe every new doctrine we hear. We must be like the folks in Berea who "searched the Scriptures daily" to check if Paul and Silas were teaching the truth (Acts 17:11). We must keep in fellowship with other believers so we can sharpen one another. It is easy to get into error when you keep to yourself. Ephesians 2:20–22 tells us that we are to be "joined together" and "built together" in order to grow into a holy temple in the Lord.

Hebrews 10:25 (ESV) reminds us about "Not neglecting to meet together, as is the habit of some, but encouraging one another, and all the more as you see the Day drawing near."

~Nancy

Can I Still Blush?

"Nor did they know how to blush" (Jeremiah 8:12 NKJV).

It is easy to become numb to the evils around us for the very reason that they are all around us! We live in a fallen world filled with the devil's perversions and all manner of abominations. But can we still blush?

We cannot control evil, but we can stay sensitive to its offensiveness. We don't want to turn into haughty prudes with hardened hearts. We pray with compassion for the lost and reach out our hand into their world of pain, but can we still blush? Evil should jar our spirits.

Have I become desensitized to the things that should make me blush as a daughter of our Holy God? Is TV constantly in the background with its lewdness and humanism seeping into the atmosphere? Could I watch this movie and be comfortable if Jesus sat beside me in the flesh? Would I lose my temper and justify it because I had a headache if God was over for dinner? Actually, He is over for dinner every night!

What do we accept through the gates of our hearts and homes that doesn't even bother us, yet should make us blush?

~Serene

We Can Choose

It is scientifically proven that feelings are chemical reactions to our circumstances. But does that mean that we are to act like animals and just go along with wherever those chemicals lead us? We are above that! We are given the ability to control our feelings. As a matter of fact, feelings can be a choice, rather than something that comes naturally. We might not always feel happy. But we can make the choice to smile. That's when the natural part comes in. When we smile, it triggers the chemicals that make us happy. We get to choose how we feel.

~Meadow

thirty-six

Overflow with Gratitude

It's easy to dwell on our problems, isn't it? It doesn't take much effort to be negative and filled with self-pity. It takes more effort to be positive and filled with gratitude. Paul encourages us in Colossians 2:7 (NASB) to "overflow with gratitude." The word "overflow" is an "over the top" word. It means "to superabound, over and above, enough and to spare."

It doesn't mean a little bit of thanksgiving and gratitude, but a great big ton of it. Gratitude to God. Gratitude to your husband. Gratitude for your children—overflowing, abounding, and spilling over.

How do you do this when you feel the opposite? You do it by faith. It is amazing how your attitude will soon line up with your actions. Try it. Enjoy a day of thanking the Lord, out loud, for every little thing.

Thank your husband for every tiny thing he does for you. Show gratitude to him when he spends time with the children. Overflow with positive words about all his good points. Constantly praise and encourage your children. Don't be meager with your gratitude. Give more than is necessary. This habit will change the attitude in your heart and the atmosphere of your home.

~Nancy

Really Real

When I bought Haven Rest (my youngest child) home from the hospital, her two-year-old sister, Breeze, was beside herself with delight. About a week later, while sitting in my lap and helping to hold her new sister, the reality of what was in her arms dawned upon her!

One of her sisters, Engedi, walked past, and she yelled out in an elated declaration of comprehension, "She's real, Gedi! She's real!" she roared happily. She repeated it over and over, throwing in another line, "She's not a dolly! She's really real."

I am inspired to reflect upon the treasures in my life that are really real. With the hum drum of daily chores and "must get done" lists, we can feel shackled. We can slip into a trance of distraction. We can lose sight of the precious "real lives" around us as we get tangled up in the trap of inanimate objects and jobs. We have to clean the house and get certain things accomplished, but I am challenged to let my family know that they are the most important, and spending time with them will never be wasted. I am reminding myself again today that they are flesh and blood and eternal souls. They are my biggest responsibility and first on my "to-do" list.

~Serene

Watch and Pray

Matthew 26:41 says, "Watch and pray that ye enter not into temptation. The spirit indeed is willing, but the flesh is weak."

If you picked up this book, you are likely very aware that the body is weak, but you have a willing spirit to change it. And don't forget the other important step—to pray that your spirit becomes more fervent than the body.

~Meadow

thirty-seven

Never Before and Never Again

My granddaughter, Chalice (Serene's daughter), loves to read George McDonald books. Today she read me a quote from him: "No man ever did the best work who copied another. Let every man work out the thing that is in him!"

God is an amazing Creator and He doesn't make clones. Every individual He has created since the beginning of time is a new and fresh revelation from His hand.

You, also, are new creation, never before or never again to be created. You will never be like someone else. You don't even have to mother like someone else.

My three married daughters, Evangeline, Pearl, and Serene, are all wonderful mothers, but each one mothers differently. They homeschool differently. They discipline differently. And neither is influenced by the other. They embrace who God created them to be.

Every one of your children is a unique individual. Each one has different gifts. Each one learns differently. They are not meant to be put in a box! The government would like the children in the state system to be influenced with their humanist and progressive agenda so they will all think alike. But God wants your children to think like Him. He has a special purpose for each one of your children. Give them freedom to be whom God created them to be. Encourage them to pursue the gifts God has given them.

We glorify God when we embrace whom He created us to be.

~Nancy

Grace in the Wilderness

In Jeremiah 31:2, God says, "The people . . . found grace in the wilderness; even Israel, when I went to cause him to rest." Are you facing a biting wind of hardship so strong it has knocked you down to your knees? If so, you are right where God wants you.

The smooth, easy road where we walk without assistance makes it too easy to get puffed up with our own self-assurance and capabilities. The only thing we are capable of doing alone is making a huge mess of things. If you have been brought to your knees, you know your weaknesses and your inability to make another step alone. You are in the perfect posture to cry out to the One who heals the brokenhearted (Isaiah 61:1) and longs to carry you in His arms (Isaiah 63:9).

Will we choose to find grace in the wilderness? It's here He gives us rest. Will we stop striving and let Him carry us? I love the words of Isaiah 46:3–4 NASB where it describes God carrying us from birth all the way to our old age: "Listen to me, O house of Jacob . . . who have been borne by me from before your birth, carried from the womb; even to your old age, I am he, and to gray hairs I will carry you!"

~Serene

God Is the Source

The cover of this book says that I am one of three generations giving wisdom. However, this wisdom is not something I can come up with myself. I can only borrow wisdom. I can agree with others, and word it in my own way, but I am not the originator. Even the wisdom I borrow is borrowed wisdom. Wisdom comes from God.

Anyone can take credit for finding wisdom. But no one can take credit for creating it. No one can but Him.

~Meadow

thirty-eight

Influencing Future Generations

Do you sometimes wonder what you are accomplishing each day? You do the same things over and over again. You deal with the constant immaturities of little ones. You wish you could be doing something more worthwhile. Dear mother, don't listen to these lies that fill your mind. You are in the most powerful career as you train the next generation. Your mothering is not only for today; it continues down the years. It continues to influence thousands of lives as your children go out into this world—sharpened, polished, filled with God's Word and the Holy Spirit.

Your influence goes on into generations. Every day you are mothering for generations to come.

Genesis 5:24 tells us that "Enoch walked with God." Even more amazingly, we read in Genesis 6:9 that "Noah walked with God." Four generations after Enoch, his great-grandson Noah is continuing in the ways of God. What a great testimony. And Noah accomplished this in an environment of corruption and violence (Genesis 6:11–13). He not only continued in the influence of his godly forefathers, but "prepared an ark for the saving of his household" (Hebrews 11:7).

Keep this vision in your heart, dear mother. Train your children each day with a generational mindset. Believe for it. Pray for it. Pray that your progeny will continue to walk with God because of your influence as a mother . . . even when you have passed on.

~Nancy

Whom Do We Trust?

Dust rises like a city on fire as thousands of stampeding hooves and massive iron wheels charge into battle. Can you imagine facing such an army? King David, the leader of the army of Israel, knew firsthand the power and might of such a force. And yet he writes in Psalm 20:7, "Some trust in chariots, and some in horses: but we will remember the name of the Lord our God."

There is nothing mightier than God. Our trust needs to stay in Him, not in anything else, even food. While we should use wisdom in our food choices and not live recklessly, He is still sovereign. If we choose a soda and fries over healthier options and expect God's blessing on that poor choice, that just might qualify as reckless living. However, to put our whole trust in something as measly as "food" is even scarier.

God numbers the days of our life. We can't put food purity up on a pedestal as the thing that has control over who lives and dies. Only our Sovereign God has the final say.

~Serene and Pearl

God Will Show You

"I will instruct thee and teach thee in the way which thou shalt go: I will guide thee with mine eye" (Psalms 32:8).

Mankind will try to instruct us to lose weight in all sorts of ways. But they may not lead us anywhere. If we keep gaining back all the weight we lose, we're just walking in circles. But when we allow God to instruct and teach us, He will show us which way to go. My Mom and Aunt's chapter in *Trim Healthy Mama*, "Food Truths from the Bible," is a refreshing example.

~Meadow

thirty-nine

His Greatest Need

As a woman, we long for love and security, but more than anything else, a man longs for respect and honor from his wife. It is a God-given instinct that we as wives need to understand. He will never be truly happy until he has it, but when he does, look out world! He will feel that he can face anything.

I'm sure not preaching to you, because I fall down on this one, too. We can love our husband, yet not show the respect and honor that he needs. The Amplified Version of Ephesians 5:33 explains it very clearly: "Let the wife see that she respects and reverences her husband (that she notices him, regards him, honors him, prefers him, venerates, and esteems him; and that she defers to him, praises him, and loves and admires him exceedingly)." What a challenge!

Honor your husband with your words and the way in which you speak to him. Honor him with the way you look at him. Honor him, for this is what you are meant to do.

Does your husband sit at the head of the table? Does he have his special chair? We show our honor in little practical things, too.

~Nancy

Designed for This Hour

My father-in-law battled lymphoma cancer at the same time my young husband fought his own battle with cancer. I prayed and felt I was trusting in God, but I confess that my anxiety, exhaustive efforts, and absolute obsession with food purity revealed the truth. I wore the burden that it was up to me to save their lives. If I did not get up at 5:00 a.m. every morning and make gallons of fresh juice, their lives would be cut short. If I bought commercial zucchinis and scrimped on the organic sprouted pumpkin seeds, I wouldn't have a husband to hold me and tuck our children into bed.

Hog wash! It was a ploy from the enemy to steal my joy and make food an idol. We do our best with a carefree trust in God, but we dare not take away from His Sovereignty. He is bigger than the GMO foods that might be laced in the potluck. He is mightier than our modern depleted soils and oceans filled with heavy metals.

He designed us for 2014, 2015, and counting! He did not choose us to live in the *Little House on the Prairie* days; that's why we are here today. with all its problems and pollutions. He has plans for you and your children to fulfill that living with cell phones cannot retract. Trust God and don't wear the burden any longer.

Jeremiah 17:5 says, "Thus saith the Lord; Cursed be the man that trusteth in man, and make the flesh his arm, and whose heart departeth from the Lord."

~Serene

Nothing Without Cost

If I never work, I will never be rewarded. If I never have enemies, I will never have something to stand up for. If I never fight, I will never triumph. If I never experience the worst, I will never appreciate the best. Good things are never free. But there is one thing we cannot earn ourselves—salvation. If Jesus had never died on earth, we would never live in Heaven.

~Meadow

.... forty ....

Boundaries Keep Us Safe

When we lived in New Zealand and then Australia, we lived by the ocean. I have always been amazed to watch the pounding waves break upon the shore and yet only come so far. God has divinely set their boundary. Even in a monster storm, the waves can only go so far. Jeremiah 5:22 says, "Fear ye not me? saith the Lord: will ye not tremble at my presence, which have placed the sand for the bound of the sea by a perpetual decree, that it cannot pass it: and though the waves thereof toss themselves, yet can they not prevail; though they roar, yet can they not pass over?" God gives boundaries in nature for our safety and blessing.

Just as we need boundaries in nature to keep us safe and secure, so we need boundaries in our personal lives, families, and the nation. Our boundaries are God's principles and laws, which He has given for the safety of our lives. When we keep within His boundaries, we live in freedom and blessing. There are also times when we reap the consequences of moving beyond God's boundaries, where we no longer have His covering and blessing, and we have to return to the fold again.

Some parents don't like to put boundaries upon their children. However, you cannot enjoy true freedom in a home that has no boundaries.

Embrace the boundaries in your own life. Teach your children the blessing of living within boundaries. They provide peace, safety, and freedom.

~Nancy

Check Your Green Barometer

Psalms 23: 2 says, "He maketh me to lie down in green pastures." Spring has arrived in full glory, and the view from Serene's windows reveals a beautiful panorama. God must love green.

While the THM plan embraces all the food groups (which include proteins, fats, and carbs), let's not forget greens! They don't make a meal alone, just like the view outside the window is only enhanced by the blue sky and the brown earth. Greens need to be paired with protein—always! But it's too easy to leave green completely out of the picture.

There are two extremes with greens. The plant-based diet theory says plants are the ultimate human fuel, and not much else is needed. The other extreme essentially replaces dietary greens with more dense food sources. But it's important to maintain nutritional balance, and so-called "rabbit food" can be the yummiest part of your meal when teamed up with the right partners.

For our lunch today we'll bed our plates with a large amount of leafy greens. Just rip or cut lots of your favorite lettuce and throw it on your plate (at least a full head of romaine is fine). We'll top this beautiful green pasture with a protein of choice. Serene has leftover chicken and salmon in the fridge. We'll be liberal with the extra virgin olive oil, add some balsamic vinegar, our favorite spices, and garnish with a little avocado and feta cheese. Enjoy a green lunch with us today!

~Serene and Pearl

Another Year of Opportunity

As I neared the age of nineteen, I wasn't thrilled about it since it wasn't the same feeling as turning eighteen when I became a legal adult. After casually sharing this feeling with my mom, she quickly corrected me. I should be excited about my birthday because it's another year that God is adding to my life!

That humbled my way of thinking. I had to agree. Every year added is a gift from the Lord, a birthday gift! He has given me the greatest gift of all. And even more inspiration comes from my Nana, who says that she would never take back any of her years, since with each year comes more wisdom.

I am thankful for two women setting righteous examples for me. And I am thankful for another year added to my life!

~Meadow

forty-one

A Returning Spirit

One of the most important attitudes we can have in our life is a "return-ing spirit." Jeremiah 5:3 tells us about the children of Israel who "refused to return," which invoked the judgment of God.

I want to have a "returning spirit" in my heart—returning back to God when I grieve the Holy Spirit, returning back to God's plumb line of truth when I get into deception, and returning back to a soft and tender spirit when my heart becomes hard.

Not only should I have a "returning spirit" toward the Lord but also toward my husband—returning to a soft a sweet spirit when I become haughty and independent and returning to a submissive spirit when I would rather do my own thing. One of the secrets of a harmonious mar-riage is to keep a "returning spirit."

God leaves us with an amazing promise in the last verse of the Old Testament: "He shall turn the heart of the fathers to the children, and the heart of the children to their fathers, lest I come and smite the earth with a curse" (Malachi 4:6). The Hebrew word is *shuv* and is translated "turn" 80 times and "return" 491 times. God's greatest longing is for a returning back to His heart for family, to see children as He sees them, and to embrace into our families the children He plans for us.

~Nancy

Was That My Lunch?

If you can't remember what you just ate because you wolfed it down so quickly, wait up! The hormone oxytocin is released when you eat a relaxing meal. Of course, life is not perfect, our days get crazy, and none of us have a full hour for every meal. But we can learn to slow down, sit down, and savor a meal whenever possible.

Oxytocin is your natural stress buster and fights all manner of disease. Eating good food in a relaxed atmosphere releases higher amounts of this hormone. The Scriptures share that Jesus and His disciples spent time relaxing at meals, and these are the times where He shared many of His precious truths. We all know that a relaxed atmosphere does not happen on its own. Get proactive!

- Sit down while you eat.
- Do your best not to multi-task.
- Think about the wonder of the flavors and the fact that you are eating.
- Chew before you swallow.
- Do your best to arrange your day so your meals and snacks do not fall at the most chaotic times.
- Avoid arguing.
- Delay disciplining children while eating—that can wait (unless there is a dire need).
- Avoid answering needless phone calls.

Try to make your next meal an occasion. If you don't remember the experience of your last meal, you'll be much more inclined to constantly graze or snack because the emotional needs of eating were not met.

~Serene and Pearl

Struggles Make Us Stronger

They say that if you're a writer, you should write every day. You don't wait for inspiration; you find it. In my situation, I am writing to encourage. But what about those days when I need encouragement myself?

Today is one of those days. Half an hour ago I walked around feeling like I was a failure. People shouldn't listen to me. How can I write positive things when I feel this negative?

But if I had it easy, no one would want to listen to me because I would have no empathy. If I face my own challenges, it's more likely others can relate. Maybe I shouldn't just write about the triumphs. Maybe I should write about the hard times, too. Maybe I should write about how they led to the triumphs!

I can pep talk myself out of it! I remind myself that this struggle will only make me stronger, just as your struggles make you stronger, too.

~*Meadow*

forty-two

The Framework

My husband, Colin, loves to ask questions when we gather together for Family Devotions each day. One of the Scriptures recently was Psalm 119:97: "O how love I thy law! It is my meditation all the day." Colin asked, "How can we meditate in the Word all the day long?"

At first, no one had a good answer as to how we could do this in the midst of a busy day with so many things to do. God wants us to work hard six days a week. He wants us to build houses, plant gardens and tend to them, have children and care for them, and "subdue and take dominion" (Jeremiah 29:4–6 and Genesis 1:28). That's a lot of work! How can you read and meditate while you are doing all this?

Serene and the children were with us, and she answered, "By sowing it into the framework of our lives." What a great answer. God's ways should be sown into every part of our lives. God does not want the spiritual separated from the practical. It is all one together. As we imbibe God's principles, we'll know how He wants us to act in every practical detail of our lives.

Sow God's Word into your own heart. Sow it into the minds and hearts of your children. This is your top priority. Unless they have God's Word as the foundation and framework of their lives, they will build on a shaky and deceptive foundation.

~Nancy

Protein Check

The THM approach is to center all meals around protein. Think of the parable of the two houses in the Bible—one was built on a rock, the other on the sand. One got swept away, and we all know which one, thanks to the Sunday School song many sang growing up: "And the house on the sand went splat!" All the children would fall to the ground at that point.

Meals that are not centered around protein don't last long—your blood sugar goes splat! Protein keeps you fuller for longer, stabilizes your blood sugar, and releases glucagon, which tempers the fat-storing hormone of insulin.

What foundation will you build your meals on today? When planning your next meal, ask yourself, "What is my protein source?"

~Serene and Pearl

Underweight, Under Weather

Many teenage girls ruin their health with "size zero" diets. Who can blame them? Runway models are supposed to be the figure of beauty, and they're skin and bone! Why wouldn't those teens set their standard to be that skinny if they think it will make them look more beautiful?

But it also makes you wonder: are we actually meant to be *that* thin? Why do we, as females, naturally have more fat cells than males? Why were we created with curves? Why is being that skinny such a dangerous place for us to be?

The bottom line is *we're not meant to be that thin.* We shouldn't be so obsessed with weight that we shred every bit of fat.

I've wrestled with those thoughts myself. The idea of being light as a feather is often very appealing to me. My scale says I'm healthy, but wouldn't I look better if I was maybe five—no seven—pounds lighter? But I need to remind myself that underweight is under the weather. Actually, we all need to remind ourselves of that.

Say it with me, "Underweight is under the weather!" Feel the freedom now?

~Meadow

forty-three

Is Meekness Weakness?

Do you think it's weak to be meek? Perhaps you could try being meek for a week! Meekness is not for weaklings. And our flesh doesn't like it. It can only be worked in us by the power of the Holy Spirit.

Meekness (to be humble and lowly) is a beautiful thing. God actually states that "He will beautify the meek with salvation" (Psalm 149:4). Meekness brings sweetness to relationships and the atmosphere of the home. It reveals the character of Jesus, who is meek and lowly (Matthew 11:29).

On the other hand, the opposite of meekness, which is stubbornness and pride, is an ugly thing. It destroys marriages and wrecks the atmosphere of the home.

Does meekness make you feel miserable? No. Isaiah 29:19 tells us that the meek increase their joy in the Lord, plus a load of other blessings. Samuel Thodey writes that "Meekness is that calmness of spirit which grows not out of reliance on self, but out of reliance on God . . . Christianity is a discipline of humility. In making men Christ-like it makes them meek."

Ask the Holy Spirit to work a spirit of meekness in you. It will bring such blessings to your marriage and home.

~Nancy

Don't Wait for Perfect

After one of our speaking events, a woman approached us to say she'd read *Trim Healthy Mama* six months ago, that the plan made total sense to her, and that she tells all her friends about it. We asked her about her own THM story—how is she doing? She mentioned they'd moved to a new farm on some acreage and they'd acquired animals, so she had not started yet. She was waiting for the right time.

We encouraged this woman that unfortunately, "the right time" never comes. There are always challenging circumstances, obstacles in the road, and new stresses to contend with. Life will always continue to throw us curve balls. We only have now with all its imperfectness. Another of our favorite sayings is: "Don't put off until tomorrow what you can do today."

~Serene and Pearl

We Can Influence the World

After God declared to Jeremiah that he had ordained him a prophet, Jeremiah spoke, "Then said I, Ah, Lord GOD! Behold I cannot speak: for I am a child. But the LORD said unto me, Say not, I am a child: for thou shalt go to all that I shall send thee, and whatsoever I command thee thou shalt speak. Be not afraid of their faces: for I am with thee to deliver thee, saith the Lord" (Jeremiah 1:6–8).

My Nana says she likes to see young people who are bold enough to shake someone's hand, look them in the eye, and say, "It's nice to meet you." How can God use youth to speak for His purposes if many of us don't even have the courage to greet others respectfully? And yes, God *does* use youth! Not only did He use Jeremiah to be a prophet, but He picked a youth to slay a giant. And maybe God could pick some of us youth again so long as we don't let the idea of youth get in our way.

~Meadow

forty-four

He Won't Let You Go

We live in a hurting world. You too may have been bruised in your spirit by your parents, your husband, or other people in your life. Jesus understands what it means to be bruised, because He was bruised for you (Isaiah 53:5). He is the One who heals the broken-hearted (Isaiah 61:1). If you are bruised and feel you cannot cope with life, remember that Jesus Christ wants to make you whole again.

Speaking of Jesus, Isaiah 42:3 says, "A bruised reed shall he not break, and the smoking flax shall he not quench." A reed is a weak and fragile plant at any time, especially a bruised reed. But, He will never crush you in your weakness. He will only heal you and make you strong. He will take you from being a crushed reed to make you a sturdy "tree of righteousness, the planting of the Lord, that he might be glorified" (Isaiah 61:3). He will make you as tall, strong, and enduring as the cedars of Lebanon.

What about the smoking flax? Is the fire that once shone brightly in your heart gone out? Or maybe it's barely smoldering. Will you let Him come into your life and stir up the smoldering flames again? He wants you to burn brightly for Him.

Because Jesus Christ lives within us by His Spirit, this should also be our attitude to others, too. We can bruise our husband and our children with hurtful words. We can dampen the flame in their hearts by careless and negative words.

Let's be like Jesus and be a flame igniter, not an extinguisher.

~Nancy

Are You Trendy?

Have you considered going grain free because the wisdom of man says this is best for your health since Grok the caveman did not eat grains? Do you think meat and dairy acidify the body and fill your arteries with plaque because some doctor said so?

Yes, certain people have real allergies and have to be dairy or gluten free, but throwing out gluten and dairy these days is all the rage. We agree that processed, hybridized bread is not healthy for the body, but there are many wonderful ancient grains that God gave as a gift to us. He ate them Himself when He walked among men. He broke bread, people!

Trends are constantly changing and time reveals their flaws. God gave all the food groups in Deuteronomy 32:13. Let's stand firm on the Word that never changes and be thankful for all the food groups—and the truth that does not change with the fleeting whims of man. Mark 13:31 reminds us that "Heaven and earth shall pass away: but my words shall not pass away."

~Serene and Pearl

I Want Non-Fans, Too

A speaker at church today said, "Before you make fans, you must have Jesus as your fan." He was speaking about how some Christian leaders in the music industry support things that aren't very Christian. How can God bless their ministry if they are against Him?

Fame can be a serious thing. Many people desire it. But they don't realize how much more pressure one has when they have thousands looking up to them. They become either a role model or a bad example.

My uncle is the manager of the Newsboys, and my Nana is the founder of a worldwide magazine ministry, *Above Rubies.* I've watched some of my closest friends get record deals, and I've watched my mom become a bestselling author. Now that I am aspiring to be an author and songwriter, I know what to expect.

Every business or celebrity wants to have fans. I do, too. But I also want to have non-fans. Or I'll feel like I never stood up for anything. I don't want to win the respect of those who completely disagree with me. I expect many people to hate what I believe. I can handle that.

Fame should not be something we seek for our pride. It should be used as a tool to win hearts to the Lord. And that can only be done when Jesus is your fan.

~*Meadow*

forty-five

I Didn't Have a Mommy

I read some time ago that "During the day, the emptiest place in America is the home." Isn't that sad? Home is God's idea. He created the home to be a nesting place for families. He created the home for the mother to build a sanctuary to Him, to fill her home with love and joy, and to nurture her children in His ways.

God loves to dwell in our homes. He isn't looking for empty homes, but homes that are filled with people and children. He loves a full house. Luke 14:27 says, "Go out into the highways and hedges, and compel them to come in that my house may be filled."

He loves babies coming into the home. It is the right and privilege of every child to be nurtured in the home. A woman shared with me how she asked her little boy why he didn't like going to daycare. He replied, "Because I didn't have a mommy." A mommy is the heart of every home.

When the children of Israel were sent into captivity in Babylon, the first thing God told them to do was to "build homes and dwell in them" (Jeremiah 29:5). That means to make life in them. An empty home can be very boring. A home filled with people—little babies, children, teens, and older people—is full of life and excitement.

~Nancy

Food for Comfort

How many times have you heard, "Eat to live, don't live to eat"? This type of mantra puts guilt and condemnation on us for finding pleasure in eating. There is nothing wrong with being comforted by food. In fact, it is perfectly natural. The first food we are designed to eat is mother's milk, but babies don't just drink for hunger; they are comforted at their mother's breast. They are nurtured, soothed, and satisfied.

God likens himself to a nursing mother in Isaiah 66:11: "That you may nurse and be satisfied from her consoling breast; that you may drink deeply with delight from her glorious abundance . . . As one whom his mother comforts, so I will comfort you." And verse 14 says, "You shall see, and your heart shall rejoice; your bones shall flourish like the grass." "

God gave us taste buds to experience delight. Relaxing and pleasurable chemicals are released in our brain when we eat. God designed our mouths with intricate sensory detections for textures and flavors. We should not have to ignore or purge the delight from the eating experience.

In marriage, the pleasures of intimacy are to be embraced and enjoyed to fullness. God smiles on that physical union! Similarly, in the area of diet, the delight of healthy food should not be frowned on.

~Serene and Pearl

You Can Overcome

The first time I watched my blood flow through the tube like my mom told me not to, I felt weaker and my head felt heavier. I stammered, "I, I, I think I'm going to faint." I hyperventilated. I lost my vision and wondered if I'd go blind. Even worse, I wondered if I would die! Trauma triggered survival mode, and the blood in my veins refused to give one more drop!

After that, I'd lie down instead of sitting up during blood tests. I didn't look, and the staff tried to distract me with conversations, but I still had panic attacks. For some silly reason, I thought a needle in my vein could kill me!

After prayer, pep talks, and telling myself, "I've had enough of this," it was time to retake the test, and for my silly little veins (and my *mind*) to be obedient. I went in without my mom this time, like a big girl. The nurses didn't try every vein in my arm, my wrist, or my ankles. The very first vein gave in willingly. I was calm. I barely flinched.

Sometimes the smallest things are the hardest to overcome. But when we do overcome them, we realize that Mount Everest is really a pebble.

~Meadow

forty-six

Sour Grapes or Sweet?

I feel very sad when I see wives and mothers with a sour face, down in the mouth, and always wearing a frown. This is not God's picture of a mother. In Psalm 128:3, God paints a picture of the wife in a home that is blessed of the Lord. It tells us that she is a "fruitful vine" in the heart of her home. Not only does she find joy in her home, but she is a fruitful vine, bringing forth luscious sweet fruit. The grapes of a wild, unpruned vine are usually bitter. The fruit of a cultivated vine is sweet.

Just as God promises that "the mountains will drip sweet wine" (Amos 9:13), which is being fulfilled today on the hills of Samaria (known as the West Bank), so we wives should drip sweet wine in our homes. We should have a sweet attitude toward our husband and sweet words coming forth from our lips.

The husband in Song of Solomon 4:11 (NET) says to his wife, "Your lips drip sweetness like the honeycomb, my bride, honey and milk are under your tongue." Dripping sweetness. Can your husband say these words to you?

Are you "sour grapes" or sweet?

~Nancy

Failures Can Shape a Bright Future!

Romans 8:28 says, "And we know that God causes all things to work together for good to those who love God, to those who are called according to His purpose."

The THM plan was birthed from all our diet failures. It only came about once we were broken and undone. We only learned nutritional wisdom because we had spent far too many years trying dead ends, approaches that could never work long term. But we can now see this THM approach would never have impacted the masses without all the crazy rabbit trails we spent years following. God made lemonade from all our lemons!

Maybe you've spent most of your life going in wrong directions. Have you failed on one diet after another? Wonderful! You've now acquired wisdom from your failures and a testimony to share with others. Don't let past failures condemn you or put you in a defeat box. Let them catapult you to higher ground.

~Serene and Pearl

The Worst is Over

At fourteen, I thought driving was freedom. At sixteen, I thought driving was the biggest challenge I would ever face in my entire life.

For a couple of years, I dubbed myself "Nervous Driver." With my learner's permit, driving on simple country roads was fine. Driving in busy towns was a nightmare. I didn't take close calls well at all. I wasn't at all what you'd call "cool, calm, and collected" behind the wheel.

I got my license at eighteen and took a friend to the movies for the first time. Getting there was easy. But driving back I almost hit a deer. I could barely see it! Was there something wrong with my headlights? They wouldn't turn on when I clicked the switch. Even the low beams seemed dimmer than they normally were.

As we headed further out of town and deeper into the dark country, my friend also sensed something was wrong. The car in front of us helped light up the road until it disappeared. Then, it was just the two of us driving very slowly, since I could only see a few feet in front of me.

When we finally reached our destination I pulled out a button that looked familiar . . . and ta-da! Let there be light!

My parents asked, "You drove all the way home with your parking lights on?" I guess I did.

"Well, you should have no problem driving now. The worst is over!" And they were right!

~Meadow

forty-seven

A Helping Hand

There are so many hurting, lonely, rejected, and sad people all around us, aren't there? And all they need is a kind and encouraging word. I think of 1 Samuel 23:16 where Jonathan "went to David in the wood and strengthened his hand in God." We all need strengthening and encouraging, especially in the ways of God. This is how we keep going as pilgrims on this earth.

It's not something we should do only when we get the urge. We are exhorted in Hebrews 3:12 to "Encourage one another daily." That means every day. Of course, you'll first start with the people in your home—your husband and children—then reach out to others outside the home. Sometimes, you have to get out of your comfortable zone and go out into the "woods" (even some place you would not normally choose) to lift up someone's heart and change their life.

Can you ask God to bring to your mind someone you can encourage today? Give them a call. Or write them a lovely card. You can text them, but there is something special about a nice card with hand-written encouragement.

Perhaps you feel need of lifting up yourself. Let me tell you a secret. The greatest way to forget your own problems is to encourage someone else. As you reach out to bless someone else, your own problems lighten.

~Nancy

Sing

Isaiah 12:2 says, "Behold God is my salvation; I will trust, and not be afraid: for The Lord JEHOVAH is my strength and my song."

If everything were perfect when Isaiah wrote this hymn, he wouldn't have needed to "not be afraid." Instead, he chose the strength of Jehovah. He chose Jehovah's song.

What is the melody of your soul? Is it a dirge because of your circumstances? We read in Hosea 15 that when God too Israel into the wilderness, "She shall sing there." Yes, you can sing in your wilderness.

Are you in a battle? Is your song one of defeat? If so, it's time to change your song. In the Bible we read of the singers going before the soldiers into battle, as in 2 Chronicles 20:22: "And when they began to sing and to praise, The Lord set ambushments against the children of Ammon, Moab, and mount Seir . . . and they were smitten." Their songs of praise brought victory over their enemies.

Sing away your problems as you sing about God's mighty power. Worship with songs of joy, and watch your circumstances change. As Psalm 98:1 encourages us to "Oh sing unto the Lord a new song; for he hath done marvelous things: his right hand, and his holy arm, hath gotten him the victory."

Are you in a dry wilderness? Is the well of your spirit all dried up? Numbers 21:17 gives us the answer—sing! "Then Israel sang this song, Spring up, O well; sing ye unto it."

~Serene

Just Straightening the Cake

Let's say you're at a party, and you're only going to have one brownie. The brownies have been cut into pieces, but they are being served in the pan they were baked in. You use the serving utensil to take your piece. But then you realize that the side of the other brownie it was attached to is not cut straight. You take the knife and make a slice until the rest of the brownies in the dish look nice and neat.

After you enjoy your piece and the slice from the other brownie, you see other people taking seconds. They won't be able to judge you. You cut another piece, but . . . oh, no! Someone made a huge crooked cut! You'd better fix that up. Your second helping might be a little bigger than you intended, but at least the dish looks clean and straight. So much for only having one brownie.

I know how ridiculous this sounds, but I've been guilty of this before and have seen others act the same. Obsessive-compulsive disorder (OCD) can also be found in ways relating to food. It's another one of those little things that we can't allow to control us.

~*Meadow*

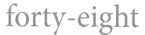

The Gathering Place

There's nothing more powerful than the family meal table. Sitting around the table together (and often including friends or lonely people) is never a waste of time. It offers opportunities for encounters with one another that you would not normally have. And best of all, it offers encounters with God.

Jesus confessed of Himself, "The Son of man is come eating and drinking" (Luke 7:34). In fact, Robert Karris writes, "In Luke's gospel, Jesus is either going to a meal, at a meal, or coming from a meal." Jesus loved to gather at the meal table. He still wants to come to your table and join you at your meal, too. Invite Him to come in. Your table becomes a royal table when you dine with the King of kings. Make time at the end of the meal to open the Bible to listen to His words and spend time in prayer together.

These times will be the greatest strengthening times of your family life. Activities, sports, and all kinds of busyness will get in the road of your gathering together. They may be good things, too. But the best thing is to gather as a family and invite God to join you. Jesus says, "Where two or three are gathered together in my name, there am I in the midst of them" (Matthew 20:18).

~Nancy

Choose Life

"I call Heaven and earth as witnesses today against you, that I have set before you life and death, blessing and cursing; therefore choose life, that both you and your descendants may live" (Deuteronomy 30:19 NKJV). While we don't want you to obsess about food perfectionism (food cheats happen now and then), the majority of your meals need to be weighed in the wisdom of this verse. Before you eat something mindlessly that can damage your body, ask yourself this question: "Am I choosing life or swallowing destruction?"

Food can tear down your life or build it up. Your choice—each time.

~Serene and Pearl

It's Not Fair

Everyone has struggles, but they're not all the same. You might wonder why God is allowing you to walk through struggles no one else is walking through. But what you may not realize is that those struggles can make you become a better person.

You might wonder why God didn't give you attractive eyes like your friend has. But what you may not realize is that you have a better complexion. Either way, you have the ability to become attractive on the inside.

You might wonder why you're not living in a bigger house like your neighbor down the road. But what you may not realize is that you have a bigger and richer-in-love family. And those things of this earth will never satisfy.

Life is not about fairness. If it were, we would expect to be paid the same amount of money from our jobs. We'd have the same sized houses, filled with the same stuff. We'd all be equally attractive in appearance, therefore having no reason to appreciate beauty. We'd have the same talents, the same knowledge, and the same old ideas. But how boring would that be!

~Meadow

forty-nine

Renewed and Refreshed

Each week in our home, we try to learn a passage of Scripture. We have currently been memorizing Psalm 19:7–11, which starts off with "The law of the Lord is perfect, converting the soul." This word "converting" is amazing. It is the Hebrew word *shuwb*, which is translated as one hundred different English words in the King James Bible. It is the same word that is used in Malachi 4:6, the prophecy about the heart of the fathers being "turned" back to understanding God's heart for children. It is the same word as Psalm 23:3, "He restores my soul."

It means to "turn back again, to restore, renew, revive, and refresh." It also means "to bring back home again." I love that, don't you? It is God's Word that brings us back home—into the fold of His will, His Word, His thoughts, and His ways. We are only truly home when we understand whom God created us to be and walk in it with all our hearts. We are "at home" when our hearts and minds are in tune with Him.

The Scriptures, accurate translation of the Bible, translates it this way, "Bringing back the being." It's easy to follow the ways of society, which are antithetical to God's ways. When we come back to God's Word, meditate in it, and embrace it, we will know who He wants us to be in our very being. And we'll have peace.

~Nancy

Don't Wear It!

Romans 8:37 says, "We are more than conquerors through him who loved us."

Have you been diagnosed with a condition? Maybe it's PCOS, food allergies, adrenal fatigue, or insulin resistance. While these conditions are real and can be challenging, don't allow these labels to rob you of hope and joy. Diagnosis can be part of the path to healing, but wearing that diagnosis like a heavy coat every day is a mental downer that only leads to more despondency.

Josie shared with us that she has one of the worst body types for holding on to weight. She'd have to try so much harder than everyone else and felt her situation was almost impossible. We asked who had given her this label. It was a doctor who probably meant well, but Josie now wore this label like she wore her own name and only saw a future of struggle and failure.

The reality is that some of us have more physical challenges than others; some have ultra-stubborn weight, so yes, there might be a longer journey to reach a goal weight. But this does not mean it cannot be an enjoyable, victorious, and even delicious path to the goal. While a diagnosis can help with direction for healing, it is not who you are and not what you have to wear mentally every day.

Josie did not know for sure that her weight loss would be slow; she had not yet even started the plan. She'd lost all hope before she began. Realism is one thing but pessimism does not help.

~Serene and Pearl

To Be Boring Is Boring

I don't know how to be bored these days, although when I was little, I used to be bored all the time.

I'd say, "Mom! I don't know what to do. Tell me what I should do!" I did not appreciate most of her ideas. I wanted to be entertained, not busy sweeping the floor or cleaning my room.

Thankfully, I grew out of this. Now that I'm older, I understand my farmer cousin Zadok, who always says, "I don't believe in boredom! People who are bored are boring." Now I look at life with a completely different view. I have so many options, it's overwhelming!

When it comes to food, many of us get bored easily, especially when we're trying to eat healthy. We only want our mouths to be entertained. In fact, I used to feel like I was living in a prison. I felt like the most unfortunate girl because of everything I *couldn't* have. But I learned to change my mindset and to think of everything I *could* have! When I think of all the combinations, the ideas are endless!

Food is not boring. It's exciting!

~Meadow

fifty

Spilling Over

God does not give us only just enough love in our hearts to survive in our relationships. Romans 5:5 tells us that "The love of God is shed abroad in our hearts by the Holy Ghost which is given unto us." The meaning of "shed abroad" is "to pour forth, to gush out, to spill." It is a "spilling over" love.

Is God's love getting out of your heart to those around you, or are you blocking it? Perhaps it is just trickling out when God wants it to pour out.

First Corinthians 13 in the Williams translation reads, "Love is so patient and so kind; Love never boils with jealously; It never boasts, is never puffed with pride; It does not act with rudeness, or insist upon its rights; It never gets provoked, it never harbors evil thoughts; Is never glad when wrong is done, But always glad when truth prevails; It bears up under anything, It exercises faith in everything, It keeps up hope in everything, It gives us power to endure in anything. Love never fails."

This is the amazing kind of love that God wants to spill over from our hearts by the power of the Holy Spirit. Our human love gives up, runs out, and doesn't have these capabilities. When people are unlovely, we find it hard to love. But you can draw from an inexhaustible well that never runs dry. By faith, draw from God's well of supernatural love that is in you because the Holy Spirit lives in you.

~Nancy

Find Your Buddy

Proverbs 27:17 reads, "Iron sharpeneth iron; so a man sharpeneth the countenance of his friend."

It has been such a fun journey doing the THM plan together as sisters. As time has progressed, even more family members have joined us along the way. In the early days of discovering how the plan works, we'd call each other on the phone to say, "Guess what I just ate!" then describe each delicious snack or meal in detail. We've leaned on each other through challenges, been honest with each other about our goal weights ("Girl, you're too skinny!"), brought on-plan treats for one another to events so we wouldn't cheat, inspired each other to exercise (or to stop over exercising), and have given each other many pep talks (or stern lectures, in love, of course). We've helped each other stand sharper against traps, fads, obsessions, and temptations.

Occasionally your THM buddy may be your husband, but more often it is a friend, a mother, a sister, or someone you dragged into the THM fold. If you don't have someone in your life to encourage you, find an online friend. So many women are eager to find an accountability partner. Walking a journey with a friend is so much richer than doing it alone. Not only can you build each other up when you're in the dumps (rather than eat donuts in commiseration), you get to celebrate the mountaintops double time!

~Serene and Pearl

True Power

People who can't control themselves seek to control others. If they can't control their temper, they use their temper as a weapon. If they miss out on the satisfaction of self-control, they have to satisfy themselves with regular control.

The greatest control is not over other people; it's over one's self. True power is our self-control.

~Meadow

fifty-one

What Kind of Apron?

I need to wear an apron when I prepare food. I am not like some women who can do messy things and still stay clean. I remember when we lived in Australia and were painting our new church. It was just as well I wore old clothes, as I got paint all over me. A friend arrived in beautiful clothes, high heels, and even a hat to match! I thought she had come to say hello. But no—she'd come to join the team. She began to paint and never got a drop of paint on her! I guess she doesn't have to wear an apron in her home.

However, there is an apron that God wants us all to wear. First Peter 5:5 (Williams) says, "You must all put on the servant's apron of humility to one another, because God opposes the haughty but bestows His unmerited favor on the humble."

When we dress each morning, it is important to also put on our "servant's apron," the apron of humility. What a mighty difference this makes in the home and in our relationships with our husband and children. It's not always easy to wear, is it? But this is the apron that makes you look the most beautiful—and it is precious in God's sight, too.

~Nancy

Back-On-Track Meal

Romans 7:15 says, "what I hate that do I." If the apostle Paul admitted to his flesh failing him, we're going to slip up, too. Most people desiring to lead healthy lives don't get up in the morning planning to grab a Coke and a Snickers bar at the gas station, but it happens. What now? Should you just write off the rest of your week? Is an "all or nothing" diet perfectionism so ruined now that persisting in the journey is not worth it? Nope. You are always just three hours from your next slimming and healthly meal.

This is not a license to cheat but a spirit of forgiveness! In Romans 6:1, Paul said, "Shall we continue in sin that grace may abound?" The answer of course is no! Paul knew it is not grace that causes us to fall; the falling part's on us! It's grace that pulls us back up.

But even though we can live in grace, the consequence to our body remains. Most cheat meals include some sort of sugar or empty starch. Your cells blow up with glucose after a blood sugar spike, and this can initiate a downward spiral of cravings.

Let your next meal on plan cleanse the excess sugars from your cells and reset your hunger hormones of insulin, leptin, and ghrelin back into balance. This kind of meal needs to be a deep "Satisfying meal" (what we call an "S meal" on plan). You need healthy fats to help curb the cravings and a healthy dose of protein. We love fried eggs in butter or coconut oil as a back-on-track meal. Or, if you are not an egg person, have a large plate of greens with a hearty portion of your favorite protein source, generous drizzles of extra virgin olive oil, a little Parmesan cheese, and a splash of balsamic vinegar.

~Serene and Pearl

Little Leads to Much

Imagine there's a cookie sitting right in front of you. It's an extra-large chocolate chip cookie fresh from the oven. (Does this sound appealing to you? It sounds ideal to me!) Take a good look at it. Suddenly you're not just craving; you're starving. You have to eat, and that cookie is calling your name!

But it will hinder your weight goals. What to do? First, you see if it's worth it. While you're making the decision whether or not to eat the cookie, you slowly break it in half. It looks gooey and chewy inside. The smell your nose is enjoying makes your tongue jealous. It *is* worth it. But just this once! After all, what can one little cookie do?

"What can one little cookie do?" Not much. What can one little cookie do if your cravings frequently get the best of you? Much.

Don't take a bite. Put it back down. Both halves! Now ask yourself that question again. Is it worth it?

If I give into my cravings instead of occasionally rewarding myself with a treat, I'll be having more than one cookie. Many cookies will lead to many pounds, which will lead to many health problems, which will lead to many regrets.

Is it *still* worth it?

~Meadow

fifty-two

More Glorious

I wonder why we live so below the life God intends for us. Jesus not only died to save us from our sin but to bring us into a far more glorious way of living like what we see in 2 Corinthians 3:7, 8: "But if the ministry of death, written and engraved on stones, was glorious, so that the children of Israel could not look steadily at the face of Moses because of the glory of his countenance, which glory was passing away, how will the ministry of the Spirit not be more glorious?"

The law came with fire, smoke, earthquake, thunder, and the "louder and louder" blast of the trumpet (Exodus 19:18, 19). It was glorious. And yet, God says the new covenant of the Holy Spirit dwelling in our hearts is more glorious! What does this say for the way I am living? I am humbled and convicted.

The mark of God upon us is not living by laws and regulations and "thou shalt not do this" and "thou shalt do that." We have come into a more glorious way. The way of the Spirit does not just keep to the letter of the law. It goes beyond the law into an abounding life of being led and filled with the Holy Spirit.

Jesus Christ paid the greatest sacrifice for us to enter into the "more glorious" life. Are you living it?

~Nancy

The Pitfalls of Pickiness

Pickiness usually starts in childhood. As soon as you see it rear its stubborn head in your children, that's the time to uproot it. If your child refuses to eat much more than mac-n-cheese, cereal, and chicken nuggets, it's time to broaden their food horizon. Picky children miss out on a robust supply of nutrients and can develop a closed-minded approach to trying new things, even in areas outside of food. We know peace is easier than a battle, but this is serious. You are going to have to wage war against your child's vulnerability to type 2 diabetes and other diseases later in life.

Ask yourself the following questions:
1. Is it okay for my child to develop a weight problem on my watch?
2. Am I fine with the fact that these inflammatory-promoting foods that my child is overdoing are a breeding ground for degenerative disease?

The rule in our homes is no complaints about healthy home-cooked meals. They may not be served up their favorite every night, but that meal may be someone else's favorite, and their turn will come. This understanding that mealtime does not always have to be "me" centered is a core value, which branches into all other areas of your life. While God gave us food for pleasure, He also gave it as medicine. There is a balance. We don't have to "adore" every morsel we eat, but as 1 Thessalonians 5:18 says, "In everything give thanks."

~*Serene and Pearl*

What if We Don't Warn?

Ezekiel 3:18 says, "When I say unto the wicked, Thou shalt surely die; and thou givest him not warning, nor speakest to warn the wicked from his wicked way, to save his life; the same wicked man shall die in his iniquity; but his blood will I require at thine hand. Yet if thou warn the wicked, and he turn not from his wickedness, nor from his wicked way, he shall die in his iniquity; but thou hast delivered thy soul." Earlier, in verse 7, we read: "But the house of Israel will not hearken unto thee; for they will not hearken unto me: for all the house of Israel are impudent and hardhearted."

God called Ezekiel to warn Israel, even when He knew they wouldn't listen. Once again, this is because God is fair. But there is another reason. If Ezekiel did not warn the wicked, and the wicked died, then the blame is on Ezekiel. But if Ezekiel did warn the wicked, yet the wicked still dies, then at least Ezekiel's own soul is delivered.

We must discern when it is time for us to stand up for truth. But we must also be obedient when the time comes. Because sometimes, when God calls us to test others, He's actually testing us.

~Meadow

············· fifty-three ·············

You'll Never Lose by Giving

Did you know that of all the animals in the world, the sheep is the greatest giver? All year the faithful sheep grows its wool, not for itself, but to give away. Once or twice a year, the sheep is sheared of all its wool. It doesn't give grudgingly but submissively and willingly.

My father, Ivan Bowen (who has passed away), was once a world-champion shearer. He and his brother Godfrey promoted the wool industry across the world. I love what my Uncle Godfrey wrote about sheep: "The soft, valuable wool, contributed so willingly by the humble sheep, who, when shorn, stripped bare, and a little cold, has given all that it has to give. And once shorn, the sheep is off again, away on the range to grow it all over again . . . The sheep makes no fuss, waits for no compliments for its wondrous fleece, because it has given as a sheep has always given, because this is what it was born for, this is what it lives for: to give willingly all that it has."

As one of God's sheep (for this is what He tenderly calls you), you were born to sacrifice, born to give, and born to give your all. And you will never lose by giving. Jesus gives us an eternal principle for ultimate living in Mark 8:35: "Whosoever will save his life, shall lose it; but whosoever shall lose his life for my sake and the gospel's, the same shall save it."

~Nancy

It's Just Inanimate

"You are a piece of stupid junk," I yelled as I banged the washing machine with my fist for the 15th time! I was wasting my voice and energy because it had no ears and heart. Once again, water was cascading out of my laundry room and onto the beautiful hardwood floors of my home.

My children saw my little hissy fit and dealt me my own medicine: "Don't worry Mommy, it's just inanimate!" "Inanimate" is a word we often use in our home as I seek to teach my children how much energy we waste over materialistic stuff.

When they complain about things like a scratch on their bike, a toy they are squabbling over, or an irreparable tear in their favorite shirt, I say, "Don't worry about it. It's just inanimate. Do you really want to waste emotional energy over a *thing*?" We don't want to become stoic, and we should be emotionally affected by what pertains to life and eternity. However, being emotionally upset by "things" that will rot in the end anyway shows we have given them too much priority.

~Serene

A New Lifestyle

Growing up, I had an abundance of favorites—chocolate milk, juice, cookies, macaroni and cheese, spaghetti, candy, and more. Maybe that's why I would spit out the bites of salad my mom gave me. It tasted different. I didn't like it.

It wasn't until my later childhood that I *had* to finish the salad on my plate. It also wasn't until my late teen years that I learned to embrace these healthy foods. Maybe I haven't completely grown up yet; I still don't like certain dressings on my salads. But I've come a long way.

Sometimes eating healthy takes you out of your comfort zone, or should I say, "comfort foods." Many people rave about the new recipes they discover, but for others, it's too different and they don't like the change. The first step is to force your way through the comfort zone of comfort foods into the real world with real foods. And eventually, you'll get used to your new lifestyle. You could be just as attached to the new one as you were to the old!

~Meadow

fifty-four

Encourage Your Soul

Life is not easy. We often go from one battle to the next, from one challenge to another. All the great saints of God in the Bible suffered hard times, but they show us how to survive.

When David was going through one of the darkest times of his life (one of them, because he went through many), his confession saved him. In 1 Samuel 30, we read the story of how David and his men came back to their city of Ziklag to find the Amalekites had destroyed their city with fire and captured all their wives and children. They wept until they had no more power to weep. In fact, David's men were in such distress, they wanted to stone him. Even in this hour of despair, he "encouraged himself in the Lord his God," and it was then that God showed him what to do (1 Samuel 30:6–18).

This was David's habit. When he was cast down and in the pits, he would speak to his soul: "Why are you in despair, my soul? Why are you disturbed within me? Hope in God! For I shall still praise Him for the saving help of His presence" (Psalm 42:5, 11; 43:5 WEB).

Take your eyes off your problems and put them on the Lord. It is then that you will hear His voice speaking to you. It's difficult to hear His "still small voice" when you are consumed with your problem.

Come on, now. Don't stay in the dungeon of self-pity. Encourage your soul in the Lord.

~Nancy

Me No Chocolate, Me No Happy

A woman denied of chocolate is a scary thing! We turn to chocolate because it makes us feel good . . . at the time. Sadly, sugar-laden chocolate bites us in the behind (literally) with extra pounds and inflames blood sugar levels. What's a girl to do? Self-control does not go far when chocolate cravings demand a fix. Skinny Chocolate to the rescue! There is no dark side to this dark chocolate—it revs your metabolism.

Skinny Chocolate

Ingredients:

¼ cup unsweetened cocoa powder * ½ cup coconut oil * 2 tsp. THM Sweet Blend (ground in a coffee grinder) * pinch of sea salt * Optional: add dash of vanilla or other extracts, or 1–2 Tbs. THM Peanut Flour

Directions:

Combine well and freeze in any type of mold (if coconut oil is hardened, bring to room temperature before stirring so it becomes liquid, or process all ingredients in food processor).

~Serene and Pearl

Getting Past Excuses

My Nana is a speaker. When I was at one of her retreats, I was particularly inspired by one speech. My light bulb flickered. It made sense. Satan will tempt us with anything, every day, to keep us from reading God's Word. He'll even tempt us with *good* things. He'll tempt us by keeping us preoccupied with our work, with our acts of service, with our relationships. That's all important! But nothing can be more important than God. If we can make room for all of those things on a day-to-day basis, then surely no day should pass when we can't make room for Him!

This often happens to me. I always find excuses. "I need to clean. I need to write. I have that party to go to. I know I haven't read my Bible yet, but it is much later than I ever planned to stay up. I need to sleep!" And while I don't want to go a day without my personal time with God, sometimes I look at reading my Bible as a chore, rather than something I want to do.

But once I do read my Bible, the chain breaks loose. I'm free. Satan failed at keeping me from God. And now that I'm spending time with Him again, I know exactly where I'm supposed to be. The more I read my Bible, the more I want to. I could read it all day.

When we get past our excuses, we experience true growth.

~Meadow

fifty-five

Full-Time Ministry for God

God is the Great Shepherd, and we are the sheep of His pasture. He wants us to shepherd our little flock the same way He shepherds His flock. God sees it as a very responsible task. When He speaks to shepherds, He says, "I will require my flock at their hand" (Ezekiel 34:10). We do not tend and shepherd our children for our sake, we do it for God's sake, and He holds us accountable.

God warned the shepherds of Israel that they were feeding themselves instead of feeding their flock. "Should not the shepherds feed the flocks?" He asks in Ezekiel 34:2. We can be tempted to feed our own desires, our own selfishness, our own covetousness for material possessions, or our own career. But God wants us to understand that our greatest career as a mother is to feed our flock.

This doesn't only mean preparing meals for them, although this is important, too. Tending a flock means we care for our children—body, soul, and spirit. We feel responsible to feed the spirit with God's Word as much as we feed their physical appetites. It means carrying them close to our heart—comforting, encouraging, leading, guiding, guarding, strengthening, and protecting. And it means constantly watching and praying over our children. *This* is full-time ministry.

~Nancy

Pining and Whining

Has God bought you to new pastures but you're still pining for the grass in old fields? Are you focusing on certain foods that you miss rather than what you can now have? God provided the children of Israel manna from Heaven, yet they whined and pined for their old foods from Egypt, the very place that had enslaved them.

You may no longer be eating your favorite boxed cereals, sugar-sweetened tea, or white crust pizza, but didn't they help to enslave your health and destroy your weight? List the foods you are enjoying now. Don't allow yourself to feel shortchanged that you no longer make a habit of those foods that were slowly killing your health. You are moving on! As the old hymn says, "Count your many blessings, name them one by one . . . and it will surprise you what the Lord has done."

~Serene and Pearl

My Body is Not My Boss

When I was all snuggled up in my cozy bed one night, ready to go to sleep, I thought, "My body is not my boss." I'm sure I had associated this thought with food, since I have often given myself pep talks at night on how to do better. A light bulb! Now all I needed to do was write it down so that I didn't forget, but I didn't want to get up!

But it came again: "My body is not my boss." I knew if I was going to preach this line, I'd better live it! My body wanted to sleep, but I knew if I didn't write this down, I'd forget it by morning. So I showed my body who was boss! I got up and I sleepily wrote it down.

Several days later, I realized there was more to this line. Yes, I have to show my body who's the boss. But am I really the boss of my body? No, I'm not. God is!

Our bodies are not even our own (1 Corinthians 6:19, 20). But we have a responsibility to take care of them.

~Meadow

fifty-six

The Family Likeness

We love it when our children look like us, don't we? We want them to show resemblance to our features and personality. Who is she or he most like, Daddy or Mommy? We always hope it's "me." This is a God-given desire. God Himself wants children in His family likeness. That's why He created us in His image.

Although this image was destroyed through sin, God is so intent on us having His family likeness that He sent His own beloved Son to die for our sins and redeem us back again to Himself. He not only redeemed us with His precious blood but comes to dwell in our hearts by His Spirit to conform us to His image. Romans 8:29 tells us that the purpose of our redemption is "to be conformed to the image of His Son, that he might be the firstborn among many brethren."

Jesus is the firstborn Son, but God wants many more sons and daughters who wear the family likeness. Are we allowing Him to conform us and mold us to His image? Or do we want to stay the same? Would we rather keep our stubborn will? It takes daily dying to the flesh to allow the Holy Spirit to make us more like Him (Romans 12:1, 2).

Hebrews 2:10 tells us that because of Jesus' suffering and death, He is "bringing many sons unto glory." Do the people around us recognize that we are one of God's children? Do they see the family likeness?

~Nancy

"Nosearexia"

We all have physical flaws. If someone looks too perfect in a magazine, their secret is now out—it is a given that they have been airbrushed. But just because we have flaws does not mean we should focus on them. While we work toward healthy goals for both the inside and outside of our bodies, we need to be careful not to get caught up with obsessing about things we wish we could change.

> Serene: *When I was about eight years old, I looked in the mirror and decided my nose was much wider than my sisters'. For years, when I looked in the mirror, all I saw was a giant schnoz! This is because all I stared at was my nose, not how it harmonized with the rest of my face.* ❃

What do you see in your mirror? Imperfections? Sure, there may be things you'd like to change, but the more you focus on them, they grow bigger than their reality.
~Serene and Pearl

You Are One of a Kind

Girls like the idea of being light as a feather. It sounds ideal and dainty. This is why our weight can make us unhappy . . . even when it's not the problem.

God made you unique. That means you will weigh differently than others. You might have a heavier or lighter bone structure than others. You might be shorter or taller than others. You might be curvier or more petite than others. You might have smaller or bigger muscles than others. Every one of those reasons influence the scale. But it doesn't all have to do with body fat.

Although I know I'm at a healthy weight, I don't even know how much I weigh right now. But there is freedom in accepting my body type.
~Meadow

fifty-seven

Which Side?

The Bible tells us that we have a war going on in our hearts. We have our fleshly nature that wants to give in to our selfish desires. If we are born again, we also have the Holy Spirit of God dwelling in us who is totally opposed to the flesh. The question is, to which one are we going to yield? The flesh? Or the Holy Spirit, who is the "flesh opposer"? He is totally antagonistic to the flesh.

Our continual choices make a huge difference in the way we live and in the atmosphere of our home. When we yield to the flesh—selfishness, anger, impatience, and the pride of life—it doesn't make a very happy atmosphere, does it? However, when we yield to the Holy Spirit, we have His power to walk in the fruits such as love, joy, long-suffering, and more.

Isn't it wonderful that we have the power of the Holy Spirit residing within us to help us combat the desires of the flesh? We could never do it on our own, but we have no excuse when we have the Holy Spirit within us.

Here's the Scripture: "But I say, live by the Spirit and you will not carry out the desires of the flesh. For the flesh has desires that are opposed to the Spirit, and the Spirit has desires that are opposed to the flesh, for these are in opposition to each other" (Galatians 5:16, 17 NET).

Make it a habit to yield to the Holy Spirit.

~Nancy

Freckle Potions

While Serene was worrying about her nose being wider than mine, I worried about my spotted skin. Serene was blessed with beautiful olive skin that shone and bronzed in the sun, while all the sun would give me was more and more brown freckles!

My thirteenth year was spent trying to come up with a multitude of potions that I hoped would miraculously remove my freckles. I'd come home from school and put an oatmeal-lemon mask on my face. Not long after I washed it off, I'd put another one on! I even saved up my dollars and bought an expensive freckle-removing, face-whitening product I saw advertised.

Sorry to say, none of those concoctions did a thing but cause me to concentrate on my freckles even more. Funny thing, after all those years of despising my skin, one of the things my husband has said he loves about me is my freckles! Now, in my mid-forties, they have faded a lot, but when I notice them after a day in the sun, all they do is make me smile.

The temptation to resist now is acquiring a shelf full of wrinkle creams. But a wrinkle or three is just part of the blessing of life. Some things we just need to get over! Change what you can, embrace what you can't, and laugh at the fact that you are flawed, yet beautiful!

~Pearl

Be Who You Are

Some might believe that every person has the same mind and that we can all be equally smart if we just try hard enough. While there is some truth in that, God has made us all unique. Albert Einstein said, "Everybody is a genius. But if you judge a fish by its ability to climb a tree, it will live its whole life believing that it is stupid." God made fish to swim and squirrels to climb trees. You never see it the other way around.

Any person can be good at math if they work hard at it. But it takes a special person to have a natural talent for it. Any person can read the whole Bible, but some people have a special understanding for a particular theme. Anyone can give, encourage, lead, and follow if they try. But not everyone is born a natural giver, encourager, leader, and follower. We should always bear all the fruits, but if God gives us one particular outstanding gift, then maybe that should be the highlight of our focus.

~Meadow

fifty-eight

Walkie Talkie

Colossians 3:17 says, "And whatsoever ye do in word or deed, do all in the name of the Lord Jesus, giving thanks to God and the Father by him." All day long, I am a walkie-talkie for God. Whatever I say and whatever I do should glorify His name including whatever I say to my husband, whatever I say to my children, and how I speak to everyone I meet out. Every time I open my mouth, I speak on His behalf, glorifying His Name all day long.

Every day we walk somewhere. We walk in our home. We walk up and down the aisles of the supermarket. We walk to places we want to go. Every step we take we take in the name of the Lord. This makes our walking supernatural. Instead of being insignificant, every step we take can be divinely anointed.

Micah 4:5 tells us that each person walks in the name of his or her god, their particular passion or interest. But, Micah confesses, "We will walk in the name of the Lord our God." Is this your confession?

As you walk each step with Him, acknowledge that He is walking with you. When God is walking with you, you can expect miracles to happen at any moment. Walk with expectancy.

~Nancy

Guard Your Rest

Hebrews 4:11 encourages, "Let us labor therefore to enter into that rest, lest any man fall after the same example of unbelief." We have to guard this rest from sabotaging thoughts of doubts, worry, and tormenting mental gymnastics. We can't be slack at this "resting" business.

I find that sometimes, I have to labor, just as we read here in Hebrews, to *stay* in God's rest. We can take hold of His perfect rest, claim freedom from our striving, and experience His peace that passes all understanding. But it has to be a daily decision. Sometimes it's a choice we have to make many times a day when the darts of fear attack us.

I must guard against the enemy taking back the ground God has helped me gain in resting in Him. When I stumble back into old thought patterns, I remember Hebrews 4:1 where it tells me, "Let us therefore fear, lest, a promise being left us of entering into his rest, any of you should seem to come short of it." The only thing I need to fear is displeasing God.

~*Serene*

The Way to Peace

Psalms 119:165 states, "Great peace have they which love thy law: and nothing shall offend them." There is more to this blessing than we realize. When we read the Hebraic definition of "peace" in this verse, which is "*shâlôm, shâlôm,*" we discover that it has more than one meaning. Among the definitions are "safe, well, happy, friendly, welfare, prosperity, fare, favor, friend, greet, (good) health, rest, salute, wholly."

This verse could mean "Great safety, great wellness, great happiness, great friendliness, great welfare, great prosperity, great fare, great favor, great friends, great greetings, great health, great rest, great salute, great wholeness have they which love thy law."

But what seems confusing is the last part of the verse: "and nothing shall offend them." When we think of offending people, we often think of crushing what they believe in. If we took the meaning of "offend" this way, we should be expected to be "offended" by sin! Why does this verse say "nothing shall offend them" instead?

By taking a look at the Hebraic definition of "offend," which is "*mikshôl, mikshôl,*" we read "a stumbling block, obstacle, enticement, (specifically an idol, scruple), caused to fall, offence, ruin."

This verse could mean "nothing shall be a stumbling block, nothing shall be an obstacle, nothing shall entice, nothing shall become their idol, nothing shall scruple, nothing shall cause them to fall, nothing shall be their offence, nothing shall ruin them."

There are more than just two reasons why everyone should love God's law.

~Meadow

fifty-nine

Life Is a Boomerang

What we say and do will always come back to us. We can't get away with anything. What we sow into our family life we will reap, not only in this life, but in generations to come. Our attitude and the words we speak (or don't speak, if it is the "silent treatment") into our husband and children's lives will reap a harvest of blessing or ultimate destruction.

Galatians 6:7 says, "Be not deceived: God is not mocked: for whatsoever a man soweth, that shall he also reap." We don't always reap immediately. Sometimes it takes years (maybe ten, twenty, or even thirty years) before the boomerang comes back, but it always does. The words of Henry Wadsworth Longfellow stand true: "Though the mills of God grind slowly; Yet they grind exceeding small; Though with patience he stands waiting, With exactness grinds he all."

We see an example of this in 2 Samuel 21 where God sent three years of famine in the time of King David. God told David it was because Saul slew the Gibeonites with whom Joshua had made a covenant not to destroy. Joshua had been dead for many years, Saul was now dead, and I guess no one remembered the covenant Joshua had made so many years ago. But God remembered, and retribution had to be made.

I have watched wives sow hate and discontentment, yet they wonder why their marriage eventually crumbles. We cannot reap a harvest of love if we don't sow love and kindness.

~Nancy

Go to Bed

Psalm 127:2 says, "For so he giveth his beloved sleep."

Our Nana always said, "The sleep hours before midnight are the best." We heard it all our lives, but now, science proves this true. If you wait too many hours after the sun goes down to go to bed, you interrupt the natural wake-sleep pattern that God designed for our bodies.

Adrenal fatigue is a modern epidemic, and the biggest blame can be placed on too many late nights. In a state of adrenal fatigue, your body cannot make sufficient amounts of the hormone cortisol because your adrenal glands have been overworked. In healthful amounts it helps energy levels, improves digestion, eases joint movement, eases inflammation, stimulates the brain and heart, and even fights certain cancers like lymphomas. But its main function is to enable us to respond to stress and then bounce back to a calm state again once the stressful situation is resolved.

Cortisol responds to light. Levels of this hormone naturally lower at night as the sun goes down and we settle in for rest. If you stay up past midnight too often using artificial light, your cortisol hormone will not turn down. Instead it cranks up and turns from a healing hormone into a catabolic hormone that breaks down the body. It ages the body more quickly and has a track record of redistributing weight to a person's middle.

Adrenal supplements and herbs may be of some benefit, but they can't hold a candle to the best remedy for this condition. Go to bed!

~Serene and Pearl

Our Greatest Craving

Life is so short. What a helpless feeling to see your last name on gravestones at the family cemetery after a funeral. Instead of thinking that life is precious, I thought, "This life is nothing. There are things I love and long for in this life. But there's also confusion, pain, and suffering. I could make all sorts of plans about what I want to do. But everything could change within a blink of an eye." There's something better than this life. Something that many of us don't want just yet, but something our spirits crave.

We try to satisfy our cravings with food, entertainment, adventures, and relationships. But in the end, they don't satisfy. What do we really want?

To be satisfied! Instead, we finish our meal and count the hours until the next. We go to the movies and immediately look forward to the next event. We're tired of staying in the same place, so we move or go on a vacation. Inevitably, we tire of that place and move on once again. We make friends, lose friends, and make more friends.

It's the mindset for those who have no other purpose in life than to satisfy a craving that will never be satisfied—but by one thing. That one thing turns our world upside down to the point where life is exciting, and Heaven is even more exciting.

We're craving Him.

~Meadow

sixty

Time for Uprooting

Through the power of the Holy Spirit, God wants to sow good things into our lives. But the enemy of the kingdom of darkness wants to sow negative things to destroy our lives. Because of sin or a variety of other life challenges, the devil sows seeds of fear, bitterness, hurt, and despair. However, these seeds are not planted by God; therefore, don't allow them to root and grow in your life. Allow the Holy Spirit to come in His mighty power and flow through your life.

In Matthew 15:13, Jesus said, "Every plant, which my heavenly Father hath not planted, shall be rooted up." Don't you love that? God didn't plant these destructive seeds. They are not from God, and therefore, you don't have to keep them! As you yield to Him, God will root up every evil seed the devil tries to plant in your life.

Let God have His way, not the devil. Don't let one little seed of bitterness or hate germinate in your life.

~*Nancy*

Smooth Is Slippery

Jeremiah 23:12 says, "Their ways shall be to them like slippery ways."

Just because something is easy or makes life smoother doesn't mean it should be done. It is easier to throw a fit than hold your temper. It is easier to hold a grudge than forgive. It is easier to judge than to search for understanding. And it is easier to grab a donut than to take the time to put a healthy snack in your purse. The smooth paths, the ones that don't require any effort or thought on our part, are slippery slopes to nowhere.

We are not advocating spending hours tied to the kitchen in manual labor, but the other extreme of kitchen abandonment is equally imbalanced. Anything worthwhile takes a little effort and some intelligent forethought. Five minutes max in the kitchen can give you a scrumptious, healthy breakfast. Ten minutes for lunch and you've got a quick slimming soup or a protein-rich salad or on-plan sandwich. Supper never requires more than thirty minutes prep for comforting goodness at night.

Some prep, some thought, some practice, and some "this is worth the effort" is the firmer path to walk on. It's not as easy nor as mindless as the slippery slope, but it's oh so rewarding!

~*Serene and Pearl*

Keep Seeking

My friend Callie asked me if I am getting revelations from writing this devotional. I paused to think about that and decided, yes, I am. I am not able to write all these devotions because I had so much knowledge before. I am writing most of these devotions because I am on a mission to find ideas. And when I seek, I find.

There is a quote I like about writers. It says, "Writers write for the same reason readers read. To find out what happens." By seeking and by teaching, I am learning.

~*Meadow*

<h1 style="text-align:center">sixty-one</h1>

You Are God's Letter

Did you know that you are a letter? You are a personal letter from God to your husband and your children. A letter to everyone you speak to and come in contact with. Who writes this letter? It is the Spirit of the living God. But He can only write on certain people.

In 2 Corinthians 3:3 (HCSB), it says, "You are Christ's letter, produced by us, not written with ink but with the Spirit of the living God—not on stone tablets but on tablets that are hearts of flesh." God has now done away with the stone tablets and He looks for hearts of flesh (Ezekiel 36:26, 27). Soft hearts. Pliable hearts. Willing hearts. When the Holy Spirit finds a soft heart, He writes in it the ways of God.

Then He wants it declared for all to read and see. The KJV says we are to be "manifestly declared." These words actually mean "to remove the lid." Are you lifting the lid on your life so that everyone around you can see what the Holy Spirit is writing on your heart? Are you blessing your family through the anointing of the Holy Spirit working in your life?

~Nancy

Honesty Check

It's nice to not have to cook sometimes and let a restaurant do all the work for you. We love eating on plan at restaurants. It's easy, too, since most sit-down restaurants naturally gear their menus around a protein source. All you have to do is choose your protein (whether it's chicken, steak, fish, another meat, or even eggs if you are out for breakfast), then add a couple of on-plan sides. Think buttered broccoli, grilled zucchini, green beans, asparagus, or a side salad, and you're cruising.

Do certain restaurants cause you to make poor choices? You can't help ordering the breaded chicken fingers and fries, and yet you keep frequenting these restaurants because you think you don't have the time to prepare meals at home? It's time to ask some honest questions. Is the drive plus the wait time really that much quicker than making a speedy meal at home? Even a drive-thru can sometimes require a ten-minute wait. It is not uncommon to wait fifteen to thirty minutes to get seated at a sit-down restaurant and another twenty minutes to get your food. You could be eating faster than that at home!

Don't tell yourself the lie that you don't have time to prepare meals at home. Enjoy restaurants, but don't let them throw you off course.

~Serene and Pearl

A Guide to the Lost

"Walk in wisdom toward them that are without, redeeming the time. Let your speech be always with grace, seasoned with salt, that ye may know how ye ought to answer every man" (Colossians 4:5, 6). The Greek meaning for "without" is not the typical meaning "to lack." It means "to be outside of a door, being 'away' or simply, 'strange.'" The Greek meaning of "salt" is figuratively or in other words, "cautiousness."

We are called to be guides and hand out directions to those who can't find the door to Christ's sanctuary. Then we will be rescuing instead of wasting precious time here on earth. We are to speak kindly and cautiously to them as we help them find their way, because we are setting examples. Only with wisdom, grace, and prudence will we be able to give correct instruction.

I also like to think of salt as enhancing flavor. Enhancing the fruits of the spirit is always a good thing.

~Meadow

sixty-two

A Holy Dwelling Place

Our God is a dwelling God. He loves to dwell with His people. He dwelt with His people in the wilderness in the most sacred place, the Holy of Holies in the tabernacle (Exodus 29:45).

Hebrews 9:1 (JBP) says, "Now the first agreement had certain rules for the service of God, and it had a sanctuary, a holy place in this world for the eternal God." Isn't that amazing? A dwelling place for God on earth.

When Jesus came and died upon the cross for our sins, the thick curtain that separated the Holy of Holies from the Holy Place was torn from top to bottom. Now Christ wants to dwell in our earthly bodies! This is even more awesome. Colossians 1:27 reminds us, "Christ in you, the hope of glory." And 1 Corinthians 6:19 says, "Your body is the temple of the Holy Spirit which is in you." The word "temple" in this Scripture is the Greek word *naos*, which is the word for the Holy of Holies! Yes, you and I are now the holy dwelling place for the eternal God on earth! If this revelation doesn't change our life, something's wrong.

Not only does He want to live in your heart, He wants to dwell in your home, too. But He can only dwell in holy places that are cleansed by the precious blood of Jesus.

Are your heart and home a dwelling place on earth for the Holy God?

~Nancy

Man's Wisdom or God's Truth?

Proverbs 14:2 reminds us that "There is a way that seemeth right unto man, but the end thereof are the ways of death."

Every different diet approach has studies and data to back up their theories; yet after years of following many of the diets, we were only broken in spirit, and both of us had serious health issues.

Serene: I had been on the ultimate, pure, plant-based diet for years including many super foods and supplements, yet I struggled with adrenal fatigue, panic attacks, and body emaciation. ❖

Pearl: I was diagnosed with fibroids after well over a decade as a vegan—the very diet often prescribed as a remedy for fibroids! I had severe migraines, anemia, and serious female bleeding issues. I had never struggled with my weight, but in my mid-thirties, I gained two sizes in one year. ❖

Once we searched the Scriptures as our physical as well as our spiritual guide, we were humbled enough to realize that even though these so-called "ultimate diets" sounded so good, they were not designed by the Creator of our bodies, and their principles did not line up with biblical truths.

We had to decide. Would we stand on God's Word where it clearly shows that all food groups are blessed and given as gifts from God? Or would we continue to believe these man-made theories that change with the trends and keep recycling themselves with new shiny titles?

We chose His truth. Science always backs it in the end. And our health bounced back!

~Serene and Pearl

Graduating from Life

Today, at my grandparents' home church, my cousin, Zadok, shared a testimony. "One of our friends just graduated," he said as though the friend had graduated from the most impressive school in the country. I kept asking silent questions before he even finished. This is the month of May.

Many youths graduate around this time. Who was it? Was it from a high school? Or was it from a college?

When he mentioned the person's name, I learned that this wasn't a youth at all, but an older man most of us were acquainted with. I learned that he had not graduated from a physical college but a spiritual school. "Becoming a Christian is like going to school. And when you go to Heaven, you graduate."

And then it hit me. God had placed a similar metaphor in both my cousin's and my mind! The difference was that while I said that you could never graduate until you knew all the answers in Heaven, my cousin finished the metaphor for me—Heaven is when you graduate!

~*Meadow*

 sixty-three

In Everything

First Thessalonians 5:18 is a daily challenge to me: "In everything give thanks, for this is the will of God in Christ Jesus concerning you." I remember the first time I really faced this challenge. I was newly married and pregnant with our first baby. Colin and I were already in full-time work for the Lord, and the mission organization we were with sent a team to the Philippines. They felt I should stay back because they did not know what circumstances would await them, but they sent my husband ahead. It would have been fine if I knew he was coming back at a certain time, but he went out not knowing when he would return! Would it be months or years?

I was devastated. I didn't weep; I heaved. I wondered when my little baby would see his father! As I cried and wallowed in self-pity, God spoke to my heart, "Do you want to do My will?" "Yes, Lord," I answered. "Then, thank Me," I heard God say. Did I want to thank God for my husband leaving? No way. However, I began to thank Him in obedience, against all my negative emotions.

As I continued to thank Him in cold-blooded faith, victory gradually came into my soul. I continued to walk in victory until the day my husband came home (which was after the baby was born, but sooner than I thought). Obedience to God's principles always brings victory.

~Nancy

Eat Fat!

Genesis 45:18 (ESV) says, "I will give you the good of the land of Egypt and you shall eat the fat of the land." Our Creator designed us to crave fat. Is our loving heavenly Father so cruel that He would give us this craving from birth but then punish us for eating it with health consequences? Healthy fats—yes, even saturated fats like butter and meat—can be part of our diet and our vitality! There are many references in the Bible to eating fat and being blessed! Jehovah Himself (in Genesis 18) ate both butter and red meat in the meal Abraham set before Him. Was He setting us a bad example? We don't think so.

Stripping the fat from all meals causes imbalances in the body, including loss of lean muscle and more fat gain around the middle. Fat prevents heavy mood swings, is essential for brain and nervous system function, it keeps skin soft and less lined, and is critical for hormone production. Best of all, fat satiates like nothing else. It gives a warm, nurtured fullness and quiets the cravings. Go fry yourself up some eggs in butter or coconut oil and enjoy that coffee with a swirl of cream.

~Serene and Pearl

Celebrate with Friends

If you want to find out who's lonely and desperate around Valentine's Day, check out any social network. Online, I discovered that many girls didn't seem excited about Valentine's Day at all. I, however, planned to make the most of this event—single or not.

I posted on Facebook:

> Why? Why, when I Google ideas for a "Single Girl's Valentine's Party," I find things like "Single Awareness Party" or "Anti-Valentine's Party"? "Single Awareness" sounds like you're desperate. "Anti-Valentine's" sounds like you're bitter and want to be left alone. Both take it to the extreme. I also read, "Reasons why every single girl hates Valentine's Day." What? This girl is single, and she loves it! I like to think: "Who knows if this is my last Valentine's Day being single? I'm going to make the most of it by celebrating it with my friends!" But I can

also look forward to when I'm no longer single and will be celebrating it differently. You can have a healthy desire without being depressed about it! Either way, I know that Valentine's Day is always going to be a good one. Have a party! Dress up, take pictures, play games, dance, eat chocolate, make crafts, and watch chick flicks! Be happy!

If the greatest career for a woman is a homemaker, we should look forward to finding the man we will spend the rest of our lives with. Always hope, pray, and wait, but never sit around and do nothing in the meantime.
~*Meadow*

sixty-four

They Would Not Be Alive!

Sitting at breakfast at a recent *Above Rubies* retreat, a mother shared with me how she and her husband were counseled to avoid having children when they first married. In the counseling session, the couple asked, "What do you think about us just trusting God?" God had been convicting them that if God was truly Lord of their lives, they should trust Him for children, too. The pastors laughed with scorn at such a preposterous idea! Siding with the devil's plan to eliminate life, they continued to provide them with information regarding all methods of birth control.

In spite of the pastors' "advice," they felt they should obey God. They later moved on from this church. Many years later, they met these pastors again at an airport as they traveled with their then-seven children to a family wedding. They greeted one another cordially as they all boarded the same plane together. However, these two pastors were very embarrassed and did not know where to look. In front of their eyes were seven delightful and beautifully behaved children—children who would not be alive if this couple had taken their advice!

Their counsel would have deprived them of these blessings, not only for the parents but also for the blessing of this world . . . and for eternity to come.

Today, these joyful parents have nine children.

~Nancy

Scared of Carbs?

In Song of Solomon 2:5 (ESV), we read, "refresh me with apples." Another dietary trap that does not line up with God's Word is the theory that we can be healthfully sustained on a constant low-carb diet. Yes, carbs are notorious for fattening people up and causing inflammatory sugar spikes, but these are situations when carbs are distorted or abused. We were designed to burn glucose (blood sugar) as fuel for our brains and our body. It releases the happy and pain-relieving neurotransmitter serotonin, revs the metabolism, and provides our muscles with energy storage.

If we deny ourselves of carbs for too long, there will be consequences. The God-given natural cravings for carbs can be so overwhelming that we're more likely to give in all at once and binge. Rather than sensibly enjoying fruit or healthy grains in moderate portions, it'll be six pieces of white bread or a bag of barbeque potato chips down the hatch!

Another repercussion is a slow metabolism. Long periods of too-few carbs take the fire out of your metabolic fuel-burning ability. The promise that you can eat cheese, bacon, cream, and steak to your heart's content and lose weight will be temporary and lead to calorie counting and having to eat less and less.

You can safely eat carbs if they are tempered with protein. Try this Orange Creamsicle Shake for your afternoon snack or breakfast!

Orange Creamsicle Shake

Ingredients:
1 orange * ½ cup 1 percent cottage cheese * ½ cup unsweetened almond milk * ¼ cup water, * ½ scoop whey protein (1½ tablespoons) * ¾ tsp. Pure Orange Extract * 3–4 tsp. THM Sweet Blend or 3–4 doonks (1/32) THM Pure Stevia Extract Powder * 1 cup ice * optional 1/3 tsp. glucomannan or xanthan gum * Optional: small handful of baby carrots for color

Directions:
Peel orange and put whole orange in blender.
Add all other ingredients, blend well, and enjoy!
~Serene and Pearl

Watch for Bucket Thoughts

My mom taught me that bucket thoughts are little worried thoughts to chuck away in the bucket. In other words, they're usually silly and not worth keeping.

When I was younger, I had many bucket thoughts. Often they would be about someone close to me that died. One day I walked over to where my mom was sitting and laid my head on her lap. She knew right away that something was bothering me.

"Is something wrong?"

"I was thinking about what would happen if you died."

"That's a bucket thought, Meadow," she explained.

There is some good in knowing that anything could happen. It makes us realize life is precious, and you should go give your mom a hug. But there's bad in bucket thoughts. They can cause us to go through life with fleshy fear and dangerous depression if we always dwell on them.

~Meadow

sixty-five

Flood Your Home with Light

What are the very first words we hear God speak in the Bible? Genesis 1:3 says, "And God said, Let there be light: and there was light." God is light. He loves the light. He lives in the light. He lights everything around Him. When He comes into our lives, He fills them with light.

Because God has filled us with His light, this should also be our passion. Loving the light. Hating the darkness.

Is there a dark place in your life? Ask God to fill it with His light. Are there places of darkness in your home? Have darkness and evil subtly intruded through the media, computers, or literature? Ask God to expose all darkness and flood your home with His light. Don't let one corner go unnoticed. When you allow evil to hide in a little corner, it will soon encroach upon the rest of the home.

Be a darkness exposer and a light flooder as in 2 Corinthians 4:6: "For God, who commanded the light to shine out of darkness, hath shined in our hearts, to give the light of the knowledge of the glory of God in the face of Jesus Christ."

~Nancy

Butter Therapy

At some point in our lives, most of us were indoctrinated with the man-made idea that butter promotes weight gain and causes heart disease. Yet butter is a biblical food. It is mentioned numerous times in Scripture, but a powerful example is in Genesis 18:8: "So Abraham took butter and milk and the calf which he had prepared and set it before them; and he stood by them under the tree while they ate." The *Strong's Concordance* actually depicts the Hebrew word "Jehovah" as the visitor Abraham fed. God ate butter! Are any of us more knowledgeable than God? Was He setting a bad example?

To help loosen the chains of the "butter is bad" theory, we encourage women to confess, "Oooh, I love me some butter!" Margarine was touted by health experts for decades as the superior option, yet butter is now shown scientifically to be a super food, while margarine is a carcinogen.

Butter is rich in antioxidants and boasts high amounts of beta carotene and selenium, which shield the body from free radical damage. It is rich in iodine, which is essential to thyroid health and protective of breast and ovarian cancers. It contains a readily absorbable form of vitamin A and is an excellent source of vitamin D, which maintains strong bones and lowers the risk of heart disease and osteoporosis.

For your health, toss your broccoli in butter and sea salt at dinner tonight. Yum!

~Serene and Pearl

Taste and See

"O taste and see that the LORD is good: blessed is the man that trusteth in Him" (Psalm 23:8).

The tongue is always curious. It wants to taste and see what food is good. But the Bible says that we are to taste and see that the LORD is good! What's more curious—the tongue, or the soul? What *should* be?

~Meadow

sixty-six

What Do You Do First?

"Let's start at the very beginning, a very good place to start," sang Julie Andrews. It's a good place for us to start, too, in every situation in life.

The first words of the Bible state, "In the beginning God." He is the "Alpha and Omega, the beginning and the end" (Revelation 1:8). Everything began with God. Your life began with God, therefore *everything* in your life should begin with God. When you have a concern about something, to whom do you turn? Do you call your friend? Do you call the doctor? Do you call a counselor? Or do you go to God first? This should be the *first* thing we do.

Psalm 119:160 tells us that God's Word is "true from the beginning." To understand truth on any subject, we must go back to the beginning. That means back to God and His Word.

We should begin our personal day with God. We should begin our family day with Family Devotions to acknowledge that He is preeminent in our home.

Wouldn't this be a good habit to get into in our lives—to begin with God in every situation? This way we'll always be on the right track!

~Nancy

Bible-Friendly Red Meat

While eating red meat is not a requirement for our THM plan, it is a biblical food that we have embraced. If you don't like it, there are plenty of other delicious ways to get ample protein. Think eggs, chicken, fish, and some cultured dairy, but just in case you are abstaining because you think it is bad for you, think again.

Deuteronomy 14:4 tell us, "These are the beasts which ye shall eat: the ox, the sheep and the goat." It doesn't say, "Well, if you must eat meat, which is second best to plant food and will clog your arteries and your colon, then do so at your own risk." No, it says you "shall" eat those particular animals.

Take lamb, for example, one of the fattiest of all red meats. God told the Israelites to eat the whole lamb on the night of the Passover. Obviously, that was a spiritual lesson first and foremost, but God is also practical. Lamb is high in vitamin B12, which supports red blood cell production and allows nerves to function properly. It is high in zinc, a mineral critical to immune function and wound healing. It is also a great source of carnisone, which is good for the heart.

The children of Israel had to go on a long journey and would need their sustenance, immune protection, and steady nerves (think of walking through a parted sea with Egyptians at your heels). Good thing God did not have a tofu alternative that Passover night.

~Serene and Pearl

Bodies Work for Souls

It's called the "Body" of Christ. You do not work for your body. Your body works for you. Think about it. What's more important? Is it the soul or the body? Any Christian would say it was the "soul." But who are we serving the most? Would every Christian still be able to say the "soul?" Our bodies carry our souls. They are the main reason we have them. Our souls tell our minds to tell our bodies what to do. When we are put here with a purpose, our bodies allow our souls to fulfill those tasks. It shouldn't be the opposite way around.

~Meadow

········· **sixty-seven** ·········

A New Habit

Every day each one of us faces challenges. It's hard not to face them when raising a family. Each child has particular needs, quirks, and a character that needs training. Sometimes we face a trauma that is too big for us to handle—sickness, or even tragedy in the family. What should we do?

I have found that the only thing I can do is look up. Look up to God and put my trust in Him. Sometimes, I may physically look up, but it is more a raising of the inward eyes to our faithful, limitless, and unchangeable God. Absolutely nothing takes Him by surprise. He can handle anything. He is bigger than the mountain that looms in front of us.

When you look at your circumstances, you crumble. When you brood over your problem, it only becomes worse. When you try to fix it with your own strength, you usually make a mess of it.

Get into the habit of looking up. Constantly raise your inward eyes to God. As you do this in the little things you face each day, you will already be in the habit when you face bigger mountains. Instead of going into stress and despair, you will have learned the secret of knowing God's calm in the midst of the storm and experiencing His rest in the midst of trauma.

~Nancy

Raw Foods Only?

One of my heaviest dietary strongholds before I found food freedom was the "raw food is better" dietary syndrome. I had learned through my many diet books that cooking destroys life in all foods and zaps them of energy, healing, and goodness.

During my mid-twenties, my husband was diagnosed with cancer at the same time my father-in-law was fighting terminal cancer. I grabbed hold of the raw food movement as a lifeline for them and for me. Yes, I prayed for their healing, but I put my trust in raw foods as healers rather than in God's sovereign plan for our lives.

I did not put one morsel of cooked food in my mouth for seven years! I kicked the oven out of our house and had seven dehydrators whirring day and night making birdseed-type meals that I hoped would keep my husband alive. Eventually, once my own health wore down from fatigue and from lack of protein, God showed me that cooked foods have their place in our diet, too. God has designed a wonderful balance for us.

Regarding manna (a perfect heavenly food), God said in Exodus 16:23: "Bake that which ye will bake today and seethe that ye will seethe." God also commanded the Levitical priests to roast meat with fire and then to eat it. Christ cooked fish and fed it to the disciples. After all those complicated books on why I should never cook food, a few simple Scriptures solved my search for truth.

~Serene

Call Upon God

Last night I witnessed someone close to me have a near-death experience. I panicked at first, and then I realized how pointless that was. I learned that yelling out someone's name doesn't always help them. But yelling out God's name just might!

And it did.

Calling on God is just as important as calling 911.

~Meadow

sixty-eight

Don't Pay This Debt!

Don't you hate being in debt? There are always so many bills to pay, and you are scrounging from here and there to pay them.

I've got some good news for you. There is one debt you don't have to pay! Oh, yes: there is great pressure on us to pay this debt, and many times we pay it unnecessarily. What is it? It is the debt to our flesh—our feelings and fleshly desires. Romans 8:12 says, "We are debtors, not to the flesh, to live after the flesh." In others words, we are not obligated to the flesh one tiny bit! You don't owe this bill.

You do not have to give into that anger! You do not have to give into bitterness and self-pity. You do not have to retort back to your husband. Instead, deny your feelings and flesh! This means to say no to it, and yield to the Holy Spirit instead. The life of Jesus, who lives in you, is filled with love, patience, long-suffering, and joy.

If only we could go through each day being reminded of this truth! What a difference it would make to the atmosphere of our home. What a difference it would make to our marriage relationship and to our children who are learning how God wants them to live.

~Nancy

Are You a Food Pharisee?

Don't become a stickler for rules to the point where your joy is gone. The Pharisees did everything perfectly, yet they did not please God. They ticked all the right boxes, but they didn't shine with the spirit of God.

Have your rules for health become so stringent that you are not fun to be around? Can you take a few days off exercise without feeling guilt or feeling like you'll have to double up next week? Are you keeping a food journal of every little morsel you eat and berating yourself if something looks less than perfect (food journals can be helpful for some, but when they cause you to be more self-obsessed, they need to go).

Are you carrying the light and liberty of health, or is it drudgery and heaviness? We are not saying to be less proactive but to continue your journey with a spirit of life, not death!

~Serene and Pearl

Friendship

I'm not here for the food.

How many people can say that? Health nuts can say it unless they're at a health-nut party! But most of the time, the food at a party is a health nut's nightmare, which means the health nut isn't there for the food. This was a revelation to me.

I remember back to several parties I attended, and food was the main thing I was excited about. Not anymore! I love food. I love to cook, but now, it's nowhere near as important to me as friendship.

Our friends should know that we enjoy their company more than what they serve.

~Meadow

sixty-nine

Feel Their Pain

Did you know that while we live in comparative ease and comfort, two hundred million Christians across the world are currently suffering from some form of persecution? And did you know that over one hundred thousand believers are murdered each year for their faith?

We dare not forget about these persecuted believers. I believe we have a responsibility to pray for them every day. If we were being persecuted, we would certainly like to know others were praying for us, wouldn't we?

As you gather your family to pray together each morning and evening, remind one another to pray for the persecuted church. Hebrews 13:3 says, "Remember them that are in bonds, as bound with them; and them which suffer adversity, as being yourselves also in the body." The NLT says, "Remember those in prison, as if you were there yourself. Remember also those being mistreated, as if you felt their pain in your own bodies." That's pretty clear, isn't it?

Check the Internet for a list of countries where believers are being persecuted—the list is too long to print here. In our home, we like to take a country where believers are persecuted and pray for it for a week before we go on to the next one.

Praying families shake the world.

~*Nancy*

Idle Hands

Proverbs 19:15 (NKJV) says, " Laziness casts one into a deep sleep, and an idle person will suffer hunger."

Pearl: *My husband just walked into the room carrying a huge peanut butter and jelly sandwich and a grin. He suggested that we write on the topic of idle hands. He'd already had a big lunch followed by a dessert (plan approved, of course), but today was his day off from working hard all week, and he found himself idle, thinking only of food.* ❋

Eating is something to do; it passes the time and can take away boredom. Snacks are important, but grazing is a trap. A practical remedy for overeating or eating when you're not truly hungry is to find a hobby that keeps your hands busy or takes you away from the refrigerator and kitchen cupboards. Reading and watching TV are usually not the best choices if mindless eating is your problem.

Evenings are a particularly dangerous time. The rush of the day is over, and you want to chill out. Knitting, crocheting, painting, making jewelry, playing the guitar, and cross-stitching are great ways to keep your hands busy. Our sister Vange is a knitting fanatic. She spins her own wool, dyes it naturally, then creates incredible clothes to give to others. We even have to remind her to eat when she's deep into a project!

Find a hobby, a new passion that does not harmonize well with nibbling on food.

~Serene and Pearl

Heavenly Music

God is the musician. We are the instruments. When we neglect His guiding hands, we have no purpose. Our existence was created to create music. When we are not creating music, all we're doing is collecting dust particles and growing more and more out of pitch.

~Meadow

A Welcome Home

A hospitable home is like God's home. A welcome home. A "let him take the water of life freely" home (Revelation 22:17). A "come to the waters" home (Isaiah 55:1).

God is a hospitable God, and He wants His heavenly home filled. He sent His only beloved Son to die and shed His blood in order to "bring many sons to glory" (Hebrew 2:10). Because He dwells in us, He wants to reveal His hospitality through us. Some people think that hospitality is for certain people who have that particular "ministry." No, hospitality is the lifestyle of the kingdom of God. It is a biblical doctrine that starts in Genesis and weaves through the pages of the Bible to Revelation. And mothers, hospitality is an extension of your mothering and homemaking ministry (1 Timothy 5:10).

Your home is your greatest place to serve God. As you open your home to the ones God lays upon your heart, you will never have another boring moment. Your home is the greatest place for people to feel the presence of God. It is the perfect place for lonely and broken-hearted people to experience God's love and encouragement.

As Peter exhorts us how to live as we get closer to the coming of the Lord, he says, "The end of all things is at hand . . . Be hospitable to one another without grumbling" (1 Peter 4:7–10).

If God lives in your home, it will be a hospitable home.

~Nancy

Contentment

Philippians 4:11 reminds us: "I have learned in whatsoever state I am, therewith to be content."

I am not quite at the place Paul was in the above Scripture, but I'm getting there. Notice Paul mentions that contentment is something he learned; it doesn't come naturally to most of us. I was known as the "dreamer" of the family, not the worker. I decided at the age of ten that when I grew up, I'd either be rich myself or marry a rich man and have a maid.

My own riches never fell into place, and I married a man with empty pockets—a wonderful, loving, family man who worked hard, usually juggling two jobs to keep us afloat.

To beat all, our first home was a tiny trailer home, about nine hundred square feet. One morning I waved goodbye to my husband, then promptly collapsed on the couch and cried. I was pregnant with my third child, feeling sick, my house was a mess, and I didn't have the energy to keep up with two young energetic children, clean, and cook healthy meals.

My one-year-old son became concerned at my crying. He toddled over and said, "Mama," hugged me, and patted me while I sniffled. Through my tears I hugged him back and watched my healthy three-year-old dance around the living room. I thought about my husband going to a job he did not like, working his weekends so I could stay at home with my little ones, and knew I was the richest woman on earth.

~Pearl

Humbly Happy

Attempting to be perfect is exhausting; accepting ourselves is freedom. But always trying to lift ourselves up, thinking we're better than everyone else, seeming perfect, and covering up our mistakes will eventually trap us like birds in a cage. Humbling ourselves, seeing others better than ourselves, admitting we have flaws, and laughing at our own mistakes will allow us to spread our wings and take off in flight. We are free when we don't care what others think.

My mom taught me to laugh at my own mistakes when I felt like crying and hiding in a cupboard instead. "Don't take life so seriously," she instructed. I knew she didn't mean to not take the serious matters seriously. She meant to not take the minor matters seriously—the worthless things, like pride.

Proverbs 16:18 says, "Pride goeth before destruction, and an haughty spirit before a fall." Proverbs 15:33 harmonizes by saying, "The fear of the LORD is the instruction of wisdom; and before honor is humility."

We must be humbled to be happy.

~Meadow

seventy-one

Keep Memories Alive

Recently we enjoyed a very special luncheon—a time to remember my mother, Joyce Bowen, who passed away fifteen years ago. My mother often wore pink and lavender clothes, so we all came dressed in something lavender or pink. I decorated with pink tableclothes and pink and lavender flowers and candles.

After a delicious lunch of soup and muffins (my mother was a great soup maker and muffin maker—always hearty, wholesome, and nutritious), we then shared memories about her. It was an emotional time of tears and laughter. Most of the granddaughters had never met "Nana Bowen," but they sat with wide eyes listening to their mothers tell wonderful stories about their great Nana.

We enjoy these memory celebrations from time to time (and for their Great-granddad Bowen and the Campbell ancestors) in order to keep them alive in the hearts of the children.

Isaiah 51:2 says, "Look unto Abraham your father, and unto Sarah that bare you . . . " It is good for us to remember those who have gone before and pass on their memories to the next generation. Would you like to plan a memory celebration in your home, too?

~Nancy

Martha Stewart Wannabe

There is a saying: "Love grows best in little houses." Maybe it's not always true, but our family flourished in our humble first home. After the birth of our third child, I felt like we were busting at the seams of our tiny trailer. I believed the reason I could not keep my house in a tidy, organized state was because we did not have enough room. In my fantasies, my larger home was always tidy, my children well-behaved, I cooked gourmet meals, and was transformed into the ultra-organized mother of the year who never lost her patience and did crafts with her children.

Eventually, we moved further out into the country, and I got exactly what I wanted—2,500 square feet on an acre lot! It felt like a castle, even though it was another trailer home, but a double-wide this time. Coming up in the world! I kept this new house perfectly tidy and even vacuumed the light colored carpet (big mistake when you have children) every single day for about two whole months.

But then, reality set in. My children were no more better behaved, I was only temporarily better organized, I kept wanting to repaint the walls, and I was exhausted from vacuuming 2,500 square feet every day. When I did crafts with the children, the homemade blue play dough ground into the light carpet, and the gingerbread houses collapsed.

Bigger homes, newer cars, more cupboard space—none of these shape us into better, kinder people. Allowing God to search our hearts, bringing our imperfections and failings before Him, and allowing Him to change us—that is how we become more like our Father.

~*Pearl*

Ageless Beauty

I don't believe it's wrong for women to make an effort to be beautiful. The Bible describes many women who were beautiful in outward appearance—and they weren't all evil, for that matter! But I do believe it's wrong to let physical beauty outshine inner beauty. As Proverbs 11:22 says, "As a jewel of gold in a swine's snout, so is a fair woman which is without discretion." The jewel is like the woman's body. It's beautiful to look at. But the swine snout is like the soul. And if the swine is one of the abominable meats that the children of Israel were told to never eat because it was un-clean, then this woman's soul must be unclean as well.

But, with discretion comes perception, intelligence, judgment, reason, and understanding—and therefore, a beautiful soul.

Besides, if our bodies come from dust and return to dust, why not focus on what is eternal?

~Meadow

seventy-two

Wash Me

What do you do when you blow it? Scream at the children? Lose your temper? Say something nasty you didn't mean to say? Or speak about someone negatively?

The wonderful news is that we have an Advocate, our precious Lord Jesus Christ who is at the right hand of God interceding for us. He is our Redeemer who shed His precious blood to cleanse us from our sins.

Instead of wallowing in guilt, cry out to the Lord for forgiveness. Ask Him to wash you with His precious blood. First John 1:7 and 9 say, "The blood of Jesus Christ his Son cleanses us from all sin . . . If we confess our sins, he is faithful and just to forgive us our sins, and to cleanse us from all unrighteousness."

Each one of us is a sinner, constantly needing the mercy of Christ. The more you keep a soft heart and seek forgiveness and cleansing, the less you will fall prey to these temptations. The more you allow Christ to work in you, the more you will be conformed to His image.

You may like to pray the prayer in Serene and Pearl's song, *Wash Me*. The chorus says, "Wash me and take this mess / As far as the east is from the west, / Wash me and take this sin, / Only You can make me pure again, / I'm inviting You to come on in and . . . Wash me!"

~*Nancy*

Here is a free download for you to sing this song with Serene and Pearl:
http://tinyurl.com/03WashMe

Front Porch Longing

I could probably write an entire devotional about contentment from living in trailer homes. God took the Israelites into the wilderness for forty years teaching and instructing them before they entered the Promised Land. While trailer living is not exactly a wilderness, it has been a place of learning and shaping for me.

I have a fear of tornadoes, yet God has taught me to trust Him more with my children's lives. My home may not stand up to high winds, but He numbers our days; a weather system cannot match His will nor his protection.

My home looks nothing like the cover of *Southern Living*, but I'm finally unashamed of His provision and His blessing. Serene and I spent five years of our lives writing the book *Trim Healthy Mama* in this home. God blessed that book and protected our thirteen children as they played outside in the woods, snakes and all, while we tried to concentrate.

I spent years drawing up plans, dreaming of a beautiful farmhouse with a front porch and a safe basement that would save us from tornadoes. That dream may actually be a reality one day, but I don't much care anymore! If He blesses our family with a new home, that is wonderful, but now I say, "God, thank You for my awesome trailer home where You have taught me so much and delivered me from shame! I'll live here happily until you are ready to move me."

What can you be thankful for today that you did not even realize was a blessing?

~Pearl

Do It Now

Do you ever hear adults say, "I wish I knew then what I know now"? We don't have to wait until our health has deteriorated to make smart health and diet choices. We can gain the knowledge *now*. Make wise choices now. This way we prevent spending out adult lives carrying around needless pounds and increasing our risk for cancer, diabetes, and all kinds of trials.

~Meadow

seventy-three

Two-and-a-Half Centuries!

Two-and-a-Half Centuries! That's a long time, isn't it? Jonadab gave certain commandments to his family that he wanted them to keep throughout all their generations and forever. Two-and-a-half centuries later, the prophet Jeremiah tested Jonadab's family! After 250 years they were still keeping to the commandments of their father to the absolute letter. Not just some of them, but every one of them—husbands, wives, sons, and daughters.

What a testimony! Can you imagine your descendants still talking about you and keeping to what you said 250 years down the line? God was so pleased with this family that He gave them a blessing that no one else in the Bible received, apart from the patriarchs, "Therefore thus saith the Lord of hosts, the God of Israel; Jonadab the son of Rechab shall not want a man to stand before me forever" (Jeremiah 35:19). It's worth reading the whole chapter.

It seems that we often fail in passing on God's ways to children in just one generation. I think of how the standard of holiness amongst God's people has degenerated even since I was a child! What about 250 years of generations?

We can't be casual about being parents. We can't let go of our convictions. We can't let the standard drop to fit in with the declining morality and tolerance of our society. We have a responsibility to keep God's Word continuing down the generations in the hearts and mouths of our progeny.

~Nancy

Feasting and Gladness

After a recent speaking engagement, we were touched by the testimony of a woman who looked like she had it all together, yet she'd secretly wrestled with inner pain and turmoil for years. To maintain her tiny figure, she'd kept her calories to less than eight hundred per day. By evening, she would end up shaking with fatigue and dangerously low blood sugar. She had young children to take care of, and her physical and mental health suffered greatly.

She shared through her tears that she is now eating real food and plenty of it on the Trim Healthy Mama (THM) plan. Her health is rebounding, her nerves are settling, her energy is climbing, and her metabolism is slowly healing. To her surprise, after several months on plan, she is able to maintain a trim figure . . . by actually eating!

The words "feasting" and "gladness" are often paired together in the Bible. Of course, the Bible cautions us against gluttony, but delicious healthy meals are a gift to be celebrated! Our bodies are designed to get hungry, fill up, get hungry again . . . and the cycle repeats. Denying yourself a healthy schedule of meals and snacks with enough fuel to leave you satisfied only leads to destruction. Rigorous calorie counting harms so many women and girls emotionally and physically.

The deceiver wants to warp the wonderful gift of mealtimes and nutritional fulfillment that God smiles on. No matter what any extreme diet says, your body needs to be fueled! Don't skip meals today. Have at least one snack. Savor your next meal with gladness! Healthy, delicious meals are not a curse to your body but a blessing!

~Serene and Pearl

His Love Letter

Saying you believe in Christ is one thing; following Him is another. It is when you follow Him will all your heart, mind, and soul that you reap the benefits. In this season of my life, I feel that I have reached a stronger relationship with my heavenly Father. And the only way I can do this is by both prayer and seeking. Seeking by actually reading and making an effort to understand the depth of the beautiful "Love Letter" He wrote for me and for you.

Read your Bible, friend. Even though I'm not always a perfect and faithful servant, I can't fully express the comfort and joy of having Jesus as my everything. As I read some of His Word tonight, my eyes filled with tears. That is the power of His Love Letter to me.

~*Meadow*

seventy-four

God Heals Broken Lives

There are so many hurting people, not only poor people who are struggling but also those who are affluent, and yet their lives are broken and crushed. Their marriages are tearing apart. And again, some of them are in the church, and sometimes, even in leadership.

And yet God is waiting to heal. He is the healer of broken lives. When Jesus went into the synagogue at Nazareth, He picked up the scroll and read from Isaiah, "The Spirit of the Lord is upon me, because he that anointed me . . . to heal the brokenhearted" (Isaiah 61:1-3 and Luke 4:16-19). The word "brokenhearted" is talking about those whose lives are shattered and broken to shivers.

You may be feeling utterly crushed. Your life is broken into little bits, and you can't imagine how to get it back together again. Dear hurting one, God is waiting to heal and restore you. Lay your life before Him and let Him come in with His light, His love, His healing balm, and His restoring anointing. He will do it, little by little, if you let Him. Allow His living Word to heal you. Your circumstances may not change right away, but God will heal your soul.

You cannot cope unless your soul is whole. Let Him come in and flood your life. His love will enable you to forgive, to let go of hurt and bitterness, and to be healed and restored. He only is the "restorer of your soul."

~Nancy

Don't Look Back!

Most of us know the story of Lot's wife in Genesis chapter 19. During her angelic rescue from a city doomed to destruction, she looked back and became a pillar of salt. She had lived in that city for years; she'd established a home and raised her children there—it held all her memories. She looked back because it was comfortable and familiar, not because it was better or safer. It was actually a dangerous place to live. Even her daughters were in danger of being corrupted and abused.

If God is equipping you with more of His knowledge on how to take care of your body and the health of your family, you are in His rescue. Do not be like Lot's wife and look back because the past is all you know. Yes, frozen, boxed lasagna is easy, familiar, and comfortable. Yes, sugar-laden sweet tea is what you were raised on. Unfortunately, both are destructive to your health goals. Embrace the new path without nostalgia.

~Serene and Pearl

Always After God's Heart

"O LORD, give ear to my supplications: in thy faithfulness answer me, and in thy righteousness" (Psalms 123:1). Prayer is the answer to everything. And by answering your problems with prayers, God answers you. But why did David ask God to "hear" his prayer when God can read the very thoughts of our minds? David was asking God to consider his prayer. For in Proverbs 15:29, it says, "The LORD is far from the wicked: but He heareth the prayer of the righteous."

God knows our prayers, but He might not always consider them. If we have left God in the ways of wickedness, then He will have to leave us. But if we are in the ways of righteousness, God will answer our prayers. Not always in the ways we want but in the ways He knows what's best for us.

How can we be sure when we are in righteousness or wickedness? The verse before 15:29 answers that question: "The heart of the righteous studieth to answer: but the mouth of the wicked poureth out evil things."

If we're really after God's heart, then we will actually make an effort.

~Meadow

seventy-five

Lift Up Your Head

Are you downcast today? There's no need to stay discouraged any longer. God is waiting to lift you up. David confessed, "But thou, O Lord, art a shield for me, my glory, and the lifter up of mine head" (Psalm 3:3). Don't forget, your confession will determine your attitude.

The word "lifter" in the Hebrew is *ruwm* and means "to be high, exalted, the state of being on a higher place, or movement in an upward direction." God's intention for you is not to be downcast, discouraged, disheartened, dejected, depressed, dispirited, dismayed, disconsolate, and down in the dumps! It's time to come *up*!

God's intention for you is to live on a higher plain—a place where you trust in His unfailing love, a place where you know beyond all shadow of doubt that God is bigger than your problem, a place where you look at your afflictions in the light of eternity, and a place where you rejoice in the Lord even when you can't rejoice in what is happening.

David again confessed in Psalm 40:2 (TLB): "He lifted me out of the pit of despair, out from the bog and the mire, and set my feet on a hard, firm path and steadied me as I walked along." David continually experienced God's lifting power and called Him the "Lifter up of mine head" (Psalm 3:3).

God is waiting to lift you up, too. Look up to Him today.

~Nancy

Tribal Wars

Psalm 133:1 says, "Behold how good and how pleasant it is for brethren to dwell together in unity."

Dietary camps can be almost as hateful as "clicks" in high school. There's the "I only cook with organic non-GMO foods" camp versus the "I'm not going to spend time nitpicking the purity of my food" camp. Things can get rather heated.

We might be sisters but we are not twins when it comes to our own approaches to preparing and enjoying food. We've realized we can't make each other's brains tick the same way as our own no matter how much we spout off about our own beliefs and try to force them on one another.

As believers, many of us have theological differences, yet we can come together under the cornerstone of our faith. Our salvation comes through Jesus Christ alone. That's what counts. All different styles of cooks and personalities can unite under core, biblical dietary principles. The smaller stuff we disagree on needn't trip us up and divide us. Instead, we can cheer one another on for our own unique styles of walking the journey.

> Serene: *Kombucha mushrooms, kefir grains, big bowls of sprouting ancient grains, fifty-gallon tubs of extra virgin coconut oil—you'll find these things in my kitchen. I go to Pearl's house and notice the microwave she uses to make her Muffin in a Mug. There's never anything sprouting on her countertop. Yes, her way is different than mine, yet she has gained health doing THM in her own way!* ❀

~Serene and Pearl

Never Be Ashamed

In 2 Timothy 1:8, 9, Paul tells Timothy, "Be not thou therefore ashamed of the testimony of our Lord, nor of me, his prisoner: but be thou partaker of the afflictions of the gospel according to the power of God; Who hath saved us, and called us with an holy calling, not according to our works, but according to his purpose and grace, which was given us in Christ Jesus before the world began."

Every Christian who has ever read this verse knows not to be ashamed of being a witness for Jesus Christ as Lord and Savior. We are not to be afraid of what others might think. Saying we are Christians is easy. Many people say they are Christians without being Christ-followers. So this verse doesn't seem hard to follow. But hold on: did not Christ come to fulfill the law and not change it? Many "Christians" believe that they only need Christ's price paid on the cross to be a Christian. But if Jesus Christ really is the Son of God, we are not to be ashamed of His testimony, old or new.

By being partakers of the afflictions of the Gospel, we should be willing to suffer in order to spread God's message—whether people want to hear it or not. Verse 9 makes the reason for that command even more clear by pointing out that God's plan is more important than our plan. God's teaching is more important than our teaching.

~*Meadow*

seventy-six

Best Health Tonic

Have you found a good health tonic? A good one is usually very expensive so that you can't afford it anyway. I have good news. I've found one that's *free*!

Better than medicine, expensive vitamins, or pep pills is a joyful heart. This is the tonic God prescribes. Proverbs 17:22 says, "A merry heart doeth good like a medicine; but a broken spirit drieth the bones."

This is easy to say when everything is rosy, but what about when we go through trouble and heartache? We can only have a joyful heart that is not dependent on circumstances when we put our trust in God, acknowledge that He is in control of every situation, and believe He is working it out for our eternal good.

Here are three more translations. Choose the one that impacts you the most, type it in large type, and pin it up on your wall to remind you.

"Being cheerful keeps you healthy, it is slow death to be gloomy all the time" (GNT). Don't you love this free tonic?

"A cheerful heart is good medicine, but a broken spirit saps a person's strength" (NLT). Our attitude either builds up our emotional and nervous system or totally drains us. Which do want?

"A cheerful disposition is good for your health, gloom and doom leave you bone-tired" (MSG). Are you feeling tired? This free tonic is the one for you.

~Nancy

The Call of the Cupboard

In a perfect world, our cupboards would not contain any unhealthy foods. But, of course, many of us cannot throw every bit of tempting junk food out of our kitchen cupboards. Not all husbands or roommates are on the same health journey as we are.

Drown out the "come hither" chant of the Doritos with a "Hallelujah Chorus" from other healthy, crunchy snacks. How about spicy nuts? You can check out lots of other great ideas from the "Snacks" chapter of the *Trim Healthy Mama* book. Don't rely on your self control; it will let you down. Rely on other healthy options.

~Serene and Pearl

Who is a Lady?

The title of *lady* used to be bestowed on women who earned civil respect. It was the feminine term for gentleman. It meant gentle*woman*. Women who respected the value of femininity, modesty, manners, morals, kindness. and a good reputation were respected themselves.

Thankfully, the meaning of gentleman is no longer old-fashioned. Women are still quick to notice the difference between a man and a gentleman. And we are quick to give those that bear that title our respect.

But "ladies" seem to receive a lot more latitude these days. A woman can publicly show off every inch of her skin, speak the language of profanity, never commit a single act of courtesy, crush someone's reputation behind their back, and *still* be called a lady.

Sometimes I wonder what our ancestors would think if they could see their children now. How did we get into such a state when we don't even respect *respect*?

~Meadow

.... seventy-seven ....

Stockpiling

Are you facing a difficult trial? Suffering an affliction? Being persecuted for walking in God's truth? Please don't despair. There is more happening behind the scenes than what you realize!

After telling the Corinthian believers about the troubles and persecutions he was facing, Paul states, "For our light affliction, which is but for a moment, worketh for us a far more exceeding and eternal weight of glory; while we look not at the things which are seen, but at the things which are not seen: for the things which are seen are temporal; but the things which are not seen are eternal" (2 Corinthians 4:16–18).

When you are going through a trial, it seems endless, but God reminds us that in the light of eternity, it's only transitory. He also reminds us that it is working for us a great reward in the eternal realm. In fact, He uses five adjectives to describe the glory that will be revealed in us. Count them— far, more, exceeding, eternal, weight of glory. The CEB translation says, "Our temporary minor problems are producing an eternal stockpile of glory for us that is beyond all comparison."

Therefore, don't keep your mind fixed on your problem. Don't let it consume you. Instead, fix your gaze on the unseen, on the eternal, on what God is working in you. The difficulty you are enduring is only temporary, but the work God is doing in you is eternal.

Are you stockpiling for glory?

~*Nancy*

Keep Your Own Vineyard

Song of Solomon 1:6 says, "They made me the keeper of the vineyards, But my own vineyard I have not kept."

Peggy approached us at a ladies' convention where we were speaking. She wanted to purchase our book for her sister who'd asked her to pick it up. Peggy looked pale with dark circles under her eyes and had a slouch to her posture. She had beautiful features, but they were shadowed with the heaviness of fatigue and some extra weight she mentioned had crept up during the last five years. We asked her if she had the book herself, and she answered that she'd never have the time to read it.

Peggy is a homeschool mom who stays up well past midnight most nights marking her children's test papers, preparing lessons, writing grocery lists and food menus, and trying to balance their household budget. We tried to speak some life into Peggy's situation and encourage her in the importance of her own health and vitality.

We shared that we are also moms of large families who homeschool but we all must make the choice on how much we take on. We have to know our limits, and more than perfectly graded papers, our children need a healthy mama. They will take away more positives from their childhood by seeing us as a good example of living life with happy energy than mere academic facts (many of which we all forget anyway).

~Serene and Pearl

Giving Recklessly

I don't know if it's because I'm one of five siblings, or being the oldest for that matter, but I hate *not* sharing! I don't always feel this way—I may not always want to share my drinks with people or offer them my plate of food when I've already double dipped. But when I buy a packet of nuts from the gas station, I usually like offering it to the people in the car. When I go on a trip away from home, I'm more excited about buying treats to bring back to my family than for myself. When I encounter a homeless man, I get a revelation that maybe God allowed me to buy some food, not for myself, but for him.

Being the oldest of five siblings, I am always asked if they can taste my treat. I am delighted to let someone experience the same taste that I am enjoying. I am always asked if they can play with my phone. They don't have their own smart phones; why should I keep mine all to myself? They always ask if they can use my guitar. Well, that's not always easy. "Please be careful with it!"

Many siblings feel they have to fight each other to get their fair share. But over the years, fairness has lost its hold on me. I don't care if they get more than I do because it's so much better to give than to receive (Acts 20:35).

~*Meadow*

seventy-eight

The Power of a Baby

Truly, God's ways are higher than our ways and His thoughts higher than our thoughts (Isaiah 55:8, 9). Who would ever dream that infants and nursing babes could defeat the enemy? And yet this is what God says in Psalm 8:2: "Out of the mouth of babes and sucklings hast thou ordained strength because of thine enemies, that thou mightest still the enemy and the avenger."

Every precious new baby that comes into the world, born in the image of God, is another opportunity to destroy the works of the devil. Even the Son of God, Creator and Ruler of the universe, came into the world as a little baby, and yet will one day bring all His enemies under His feet.

J. J. Stewart Perowne translates Psalm 8:2: "Out of the mouth even of lisping children Thou hast founded strength; Thou hast made them a bulwark or defence against those who rebel against Thee; with their praises and confessions Thou puttest to silence the malicious slanders of Thy enemies."

I love the words of Frank Boreham: "We fancy that God can only manage His world by big battalions abroad, when all the while He is doing it by beautiful babies at home. When a wrong wants righting, or a truth wants preaching, or a continent wants opening, God sends a baby into the world to do it. That is why, long ago, a babe was born in Bethlehem."

Truly, God's ways are higher than our ways.

~Nancy

Late Night Munchies

Struggling with the super munchies at night? Another reason to get to bed earlier! If you are often up until midnight, your body will beg you for more food just to manage to stay awake. Too often it is not a safe or regular hungry feeling but a ravenous fridge searching instinct that seeks only the foods classified as no no's for late night eating. But even if you attempt to stick to THM foods, it seems to be the really rich, decadent stuff that ends up being gobbled because when we are ultra-fatigued we lose our common sense.

If you are truly, extremely hungry in the evening and there's no way around staying up later—lighter snacks are your best option. Heavy snacks right before bed offer your body too many calories when all your body will be doing is sleeping. If your body is really screaming for a snack try our Cottage Berry Whip recipe.

Cottage Berry Whip
Ingredients:
½ cup frozen berries * ½ cup low fat cottage cheese * 2-3 tsp. THM Sweet Blend or 2-3 doonks THM Stevia Extract Powder

Directions:
Place all ingredients in a food processor and process well.

Note. It is important to realize that the different seasons of our lives call for different leniencies with night time snacking. If you are post-menopausal, you may have an even harder time losing weight if heavy snacks are eaten in the evening due to metabolism slowdown from lost hormones. If you do have to snack, it will be better as a lighter option. On the other spectrum, younger women who are either nursing through the night or pregnant will definitely need an evening snack that is protein rich.

Let Them Know You Care

How can I sit in my seat and watch a child lie in the grass in pain after falling off his bike? "Oh, I guess he didn't break any bones. He probably only twisted his leg or earned a few scrapes. He is probably fine." His *body* is probably fine. But is his mind?

Is he wondering why I am not rushing to him to ask the simple question, "Are you okay?" just to make sure? Does he think I don't care? That no one cares?

Sometimes we forget the importance of empathy. If we don't receive sympathy in times of pain, both physically and mentally, it can be more painful than the original pain itself, because those are the times we either feel loved and cared for by the people around us or the times we feel the most alone.

Even if we are assured by others that someone is okay, that they need their space and need to learn how to handle their problems on their own, never ignore the little feeling inside that calls you to their aid. Sometimes, empathy can be the Band-Aid—or even the cure—that lets him know he matters.

~Meadow

seventy-nine

Outspoken for the Truth

Our Christian walk is not only believing in Jesus Christ but confessing that He is our Lord and Savior (Romans 10:9, 10). We are only born again by believing and confessing. This is the way we continue to walk in Christ. Every new understanding of truth we receive, we must also confess.

Hebrews 10:35 says, "Cast not away therefore your confidence, which hath great recompense of reward." The Greek word for "confidence" is *parrhesia*; it actually means "all out-spokenness—frankness, bluntness, publically and boldly speaking, assurance." We do not hide our salvation; we proclaim it. We do not hide the truth God reveals to us; we boldly speak it out, even in the face of ridicule and resistance from family and those around us.

Confession keeps our faith real. Confession keeps truth vibrant in our hearts. The more you share truth with others, the more it becomes part of your life.

This same word is used by Jesus, the early disciples, and by Paul speaking boldly. Paul and Barnabas "waxed bold" in the midst of people who were "contradicting and blaspheming" them (Acts 13:45, 46).

Our confession may get us into trouble, but do we stop confessing? We dare not! We had better start boldly confessing the truth more than ever, because we don't know how much longer we will be able to do it without real persecution! A new day has dawned in America. It's time for God's people to be more outspoken than ever!

~Nancy

Open Your Mind, Open Your Palate!

It is not only children who are picky eaters. We receive many e-mails from people asking if our plan will work for them since they don't eat certain things. They're picky, not because of allergies or religious convictions, but just because. We are not saying everybody has to like every food or every flavor, as we all have our natural preferences. But if the only veggie you can tolerate is a potato, there is big room for progress.

As long as you are breathing, you can change! The Scriptures call us "new creatures in Christ." This means old ideas and habits do not have to control your future. Don't give up on certain healthy foods if you've tried them only once or twice. Be creative. Experiment. One flop with a recipe does not mean you should never try it again.

Don't like broccoli? Melt butter all over it, season it generously with sea salt and pepper, and grate a little cheese over the top. Open your mind. Taste without your preconceived notions telling you it is gross. This is miracle food for your body. Allow your taste buds to capture the magic!

~Serene and Pearl

Are We Sharing the Gospel?

"God is fair." I am in awestruck wonder as I study the book of Ezekiel. I thought of this book recently as I spoke this sentence to a family friend in agreement. Not as many Christians care about sharing the Gospel these days. But why, when we are *called* to? Ezekiel was called to warn Israel of their sin even when God knew they would only continue to reject Him. Why did God even bother? Because God is fair! He gave them a chance to be warned before they were punished.

My friend enlightened the revelation even further with a metaphor. Say God had four children, and He clothed, sheltered, and taught only two of His children, but He didn't care about the other two. What kind of loving Father is that? A loving Father cares about *all* of his children.

"Do you know how many people in this world have not even heard of the Gospel?" he asked me. I learned that 32 percent of the world's population has no opportunity to hear the Gospel. A whopping 680 million don't even know who Jesus is, and 66,000 of these people die each day—never knowing.

"Many people know that God is love, mercy, and kindness . . . but they forget one thing. He is also equity," he continued.

"For God so loved the whole world that he gave His only son" (John 3:16). Everyone deserves to hear the Gospel, even if they won't accept it.

~Meadow

eighty

Truth Seekers

I long for God to lead me into truth and expose all deception in my life. I hate deception and pant for truth.

Because God is truth and can't be anything other than truth, He hates lies. I want to be in sync with God, which means I must immerse myself in His Word. Man's humanistic reasoning is no match for God's eternal truth. However, it is only when we know His truth that we discern deception.

When the Jews were taken captive to Babylon, God warned them to watch out for deception "in the midst of you" (Jeremiah 29:8, 9). You would have thought He would have warned them to watch out for the deception and confusion in Babylon. However, He knew they would see through that because it was so blatant. The deception we have to be concerned about is that which is so similar to the truth that it takes being filled with God's Word and the Holy Spirit to discern it!

I want to be a truth-seeker, truth-finder, truth-lover, truth-embracer, truth-adherer, truth-speaker, and truth-promoter! Don't you?

And let's raise children who have a love for truth: children who will not be swayed by humanistic propaganda, children who can discern the difference between good and evil, and children who will be able to stand, "and having done all, to stand" against all deception and evil (Ephesians 6:13).

~Nancy

The Health Foody Trap

Proverbs 23:1–3 NIV says, "When you sit to dine with a ruler, note well what is before you, and put a knife to your throat if you are given to gluttony. Do not crave his delicacies, for that food is deceptive."

Not many of us sit down with rulers, but we can still heed the lesson here: some foods are deceptive. Just because you can buy it in health food store and the packaging says *organic* or *non-GMO* or *gluten-free*, it does not mean this product will do your body any good. Most of the bars that fill health food shelves are as hard on your blood sugar as those in the candy aisle of Walmart. They may have more nutrients, but the way they spike blood sugar with organic cane or rice syrup, fruit juice concentrate, agave nectar, or condensed dried fruits along with high-glycemic grains undoes the extra vitamins and minerals offered.

Beware of super food drinks touting the slimming powers of wheat grass, mangosteen, and acai. Yes, those supplements are spectacular for your health, but when they come in a base of apple or pineapple juice concentrate (or even fresh-squeezed juice), you might as well be drinking sugar-sweetened soda. Fruit is great, but extracted from its fiber, it can be hazardous to balanced blood sugar levels for most of us insulin-resistant adults. It takes three or four apples to make one glass of juice. That is liquid sugar immediately igniting your blood stream. The path to true health starts with balanced blood sugar.

~Serene and Pearl

Never Finished Studying

"Study to shew thyself approved unto God, a workman that needeth not to be ashamed, rightly dividing the word of truth," says 2 Timothy 2:15.

After graduating high school, I'd be asked, "Studying what? I thought you graduated."

"I did. But you can never graduate from the Bible."

No one is ever *finished* with Bible study, even if they read the Bible the whole way through. No one has ever *graduated* from Bible study, even if they took a four-year college course on Bibliology. And most certainly, no one is getting *enough* Bible study, especially if the only way they get it is once a week in church.

I like to think of the Bible as a jigsaw puzzle, except the Bible is the biggest jigsaw puzzle in the world. It's impossible to put all the pieces together in this lifetime. We have to wait until the next one to find the missing pieces. But in the meantime, we try to put together as many pieces as we can, and we get an idea, or as the Bible calls it, "a shadow," of things to come.

~*Meadow*

eighty-one

Do You Finish Your Meal?

It is interesting to hear the different names families use for their gathering together to pray and read God's Word together. In our home, we call it "Family Devotions." Originally it was called the "Family Altar," which comes from Leviticus 6:8–13 in which God commanded that the fire upon the altar must never go out. The only way they could keep it going was to tend to it two times a day. Here, God established the "Morning and Evening Principle" of gathering twice a day to pray and worship together. As we establish this in our home, we keep the fire of God burning in all our hearts. We don't want the flame to go out in our own lives, or in any of our children's lives, do we?

I heard a very interesting name when I was speaking at an *Above Rubies* conference in Belgium recently. A Dutch lady told me that growing up in the Netherlands they called it "Finishing Up the Meal." I had never heard that expression before, but I think it's a very good one.

We have not finished our meal if we only feed the body. The purpose of our family meal is to feed the body, soul, and spirit. It is even more important to feed the inner man. If we leave the table before feeding the spirits of our children with God's Living Word, we leave the table only half finished!

Do you finish up the meal at your table?

~Nancy

To find out more about the "Morning and Evening Principle" go to:
http://aboverubies.org/morning-evening-principle

Coffee Indulgence

A steamy cup of creamy coffee . . . ahh! What could be better? Poor coffee was made to be evil along with other innocents like butter and red meat. Coffee hatred was a fad and had its season in the sun. Now science shows it can positively increase health and happiness. It lessens the chance of Parkinson's disease and even elevates dopamine levels, which contributes to happiness. It has anti-cancer abilities which studies show help defeat tumors in ovarian, colon, and liver cancers. Numerous studies indicate that coffee consumption is associated with a sharply reduced risk of developing type 2 diabetes, including an eighteen-year follow-up study on Swedish women released in *Journal of Internal Medicine* in 2004.

Serene: Coffee still gets a lot of blame in the area of adrenal fatigue. Those suffering with this condition are told to stay far away from coffee. However, my adrenals healed the year I decided to start drinking coffee! Coffee only harms adrenals when it is abused, overused, and prevents rest. Drinking my daily cup of coffee is an oasis of rest in my crazy, chaotic life. My adrenals healed once I learned to give over so many of my anxieties to God. This inner rest of my soul helped heal my body along with a protein-based, blood-sugar-friendly diet.
Enjoy your coffee. ❖

~Serene and Pearl

Every Joint Supplying

"For to one is given by the Spirit the word of wisdom; to another the word of knowledge by the same Spirit; To another faith by the same Spirit; to another the gifts of healing by the same Spirit; To another the working of miracles; to another prophecy; to another discerning of spirits, to another divers kinds of tongues; to another the interpretation of tongues: But all these worketh that one and the selfsame Spirit, dividing to every man severally as he will. For as the body is one, and hath many members, and all the members of that one body, being many, are one body: so also is Christ" (1 Corinthians 12:8–12).

If there was only one person in the world, the world would be bland like flour by itself, sugar by itself, an egg by itself, oil by itself, or cocoa by itself. But put those ingredients together in the right steps, and you turn bland into a delicious chocolate chip cookie! (Excuse me, I mean almond flour and stevia to make an S Chocolate Chip Cookie).

Some people are practical like almond flour. Others are sweet like stevia. Some carry the strength like the protein in an egg. Others are rich in wisdom and knowledge like oil. And some have creative ideas and outgoing personalities like cocoa. But what good are we by ourselves? Together we make the cookie. Together we make the *body*. It takes all types to make the world go round.

~*Meadow*

eighty-two

Seared Hearts

I love the story where a stranger comes alongside the two disciples who were walking dejectedly back to their home in Emmaus. They were disillusioned. They thought Jesus would have delivered them from the tyranny of the Romans. But instead, he was dead.

The stranger draws near and begins to talk to them. They don't know who He is, but as He reveals God's plan for a Savior from the Old Testament Scriptures, their hearts "burned" within them. Later, after they recognized it was Jesus, "They said one to another, Did not our heart burn within us, while he talked with us by the way, and while he opened to us the Scriptures?" (Luke 24:32). Their hearts were actually "on fire."

Ask Jesus to draw near to you. As you meditate on the Scriptures, ask the Holy Spirit to sear them into your heart and mind so they will become flesh and blood in your life. As the rancher brands his cattle to place his ownership on them, so you will be indelibly branded with God's Word that wherever you go and whatever you do, all will know to whom you belong! You will be so identified with His truth that you will always recognize deception. Your heart will be so seared with the revelation of His truth that all other pursuits of knowledge will seem empty.

And what about your children? Are you daily penetrating God's Word into their hearts so they will also be seared with His truth? If so, then nothing—neither conflict, disappointment, persecution, or opposition—will ever cause them to turn away from their unflinching commitment to Christ and His truth.

~Nancy

One Life, One Shot!

Here's another saying our mother pinned up on our wall:

Only one life, 'twill soon be past,
Only what's done for Christ will last.

Will we allow the physical burdens of weight and ill health to rob us of the energy and ability to make a difference for God's kingdom? If it requires enormous effort just to drag yourself through the day, you'll have nothing left for God-given dreams. Some people have no choice with physical afflictions beyond their control, but if your malaise is self-afflicted by bad habits, then you are blessed with the ability to change.

Shana has become a sweet friend of ours. While she is joyous about the fifty pounds she has shed, she's even more excited to realize she can now fulfill the dreams God placed in her heart as a young girl. Before, she could barely make it through the day. Now she has begun the process to foster and adopt children, a dream that she'd put on the shelf, never thinking she'd have the strength of mind or body to undertake.

~Serene and Pearl

Out of Sight, Out of Mind

Jesus advised in Matthew 18:9 that if "Your eye causes you to sin, tear it out and throw it away." I have taken this advice on a less extreme level when relating to food. I don't tear out my eye. But sometimes, I hide the peanuts from myself—and then I forget about them. Out of sight is out of mind.

~Meadow

eighty-three

Investing for Eternity

Our days are filled with so much to do. We are each working toward something, investing in our passion. Therefore, we need to ask an important question: is my investment secure?

Jesus told the story of the rich farmer who had such great riches that he built bigger barns. What was God's response? Luke 12:20, 21 (ESV) says, "'Fool! this night your soul is required of you, and the things you have prepared, whose will they be?' So is the one who lays up treasure for himself and is not rich toward God."

What was the root of his problem? He was laying up treasure for himself! He was putting all his time and effort into "uncertain riches" that will not last.

It's easy to get caught up with investing all our time and effort into that which doesn't last. We can become self-serving instead of serving, but self-serving is like a vapor that passes away. Jesus showed us what lasts when He said, "For whosoever will save his life shall lose it; but whosoever shall lose his life for my sake and the gospel's, the same shall save it" (Mark 8:35).

Our society pressures women to leave mothering in the home for jobs and careers outside the home. You can't take your career into eternity with you, but you can take your mothering. Every child God gives you is an eternal soul that will live forever. You are molding children for eternity. You are investing in a career that lasts.

~*Nancy*

Free to Fly!

Walking out of our favorite coffee shop, we bumped into someone who recognized us as the authors of *Trim Healthy Mama*. Leanne was so excited to share her good news with us, she could hardly contain herself. Weight had never been her struggle. She was one of the people most of us consider lucky, blessed with a super high metabolism. But she'd lived with extreme exhaustion for years. She could not function without a nap every day, which took a good chunk of time out of her life and dictated that everything revolve around that nap time.

Despite her slender frame, she admitted she'd been a slave to sugar and empty starches. Once she'd finally learned to balance her blood sugar, she noticed energy creeping back into her body. She slowly but steadily began recharging. Tears filled her eyes as she shared that now, instead of napping, she was learning an instrument—one of her lifelong dreams!

You are a creative person, made in God's image. He has wonderful things for you yet.

~*Serene and Pearl*

Evidence Is Everywhere

Recently I wrote an allegory: "*In the beginning* was a woman called *Sarah*. She didn't believe in the original *Sarah* because she didn't believe in God. Although she studied B.C. history, the origin of her name was a mystery. But she believed anyone who said otherwise *had no eyes to see and no ears to hear. By the sweat of her brow,* she shared the *gospel* of atheism with those of *little faith*. She met a man named *David* who also had a mysterious name. When the two of a *broken heart* both became each other's *apple of the eye,* they got married in a *church*. After becoming *one flesh* they brought forth children of their own *flesh and blood*. They knew by how they would *train up a child,* they'd also *reap what they sow. Sunrise to sunset,* they *put their house in order,* and *taught them diligently* the ways of the atheists. There would be *no root of the matter* of any idea from the Bible if they had to conceal it by the *skin of their teeth*. Their children grew up in the *nurture and admonition* of *man's wisdom* by their *labor of love*."

It really is foolish to believe there's no God. Yet, even a culture gone

Come Over to Dinner!

An invitation to dinner can often create two different reactions:

1. "I have no choice. I'm not going to offend our friends. Homemade lasagna, here I come. Jill is famous for her garlic bread. No way am I missing out on that or on her homemade double-fudge brownies with ice cream."

2. "Oh no! Jill's food is completely off plan and will ruin all my hard work. Maybe I shouldn't go; she thinks I'm crazy anyway for carrying stevia in my purse. If I eat her lasagna, I'll have to work out for an extra hour tomorrow and eat only light foods for the rest of the week."

If your reaction is number one, it's okay to have a complete cheat meal now and then. But if you are scheming ways to get invited over to Jill's house every week, then you may need to look at livening up your own home while keeping it healthy, of course!

If your reaction is more like number two, loosen up! One meal is not going to destroy anything. Don't allow the purity of your diet to make you reclusive.

There is an easy solution for both women here. Take a big salad that you can make a large part of your plate and a scrumptious dessert that people won't be able to believe is good for you. Don't be rude. Eat a little of Jill's lasagna, but you don't make it the biggest part of your meal.

You never know: the dessert may be the key that opens the door to a healthier life plan for Jill, too.

~Serene and Pearl

Two Songs

It's interesting that my last song and my most recent song contradict each other. I recently wrote *"Never Bloom Before It's Spring"* about waiting. My latest song *"We're Not Promised Tomorrow"* is about not hesitating. I guess you could say that they balance each other out.

In life, we need to learn when and how to do both. Part of walking in the Lord's will is being patient and going with the flow. And part of it is working hard to get the job done. We need to discern when which of these two options fits the situation best.

There is a time and a place for both of them.

~*Meadow*

eighty-six

Family Vexations

We all face vexations from time to time in our family lives. There can be a reason. God told the Israelites in Numbers 33:55, "If you will not drive out the inhabitants of the land from before you; then it shall come to pass, that those which ye let remain of them shall be pricks in your eyes, and thorns in your sides, and shall vex you in the land where ye dwell."

When you face rebellion and worldliness, don't put up with them. Don't let them linger and hope they'll disappear. All your hoping won't make them go away. You need to talk and pray with your husband for wisdom on how to deal with them. You must take authority in the power of prayer. You must deal severely with all evil and not allow one vestige of it in your home.

It can often be difficult to make a scene and deal with something as we know we should. We'd rather not rock the boat. But if you don't, the problems will continually vex you. They will be like splinters in your eyes and thorns in your side. The problems will multiply. The enemy will take hold more and more!

Commenting on this Scripture, Matthew Henry says, "If we do not drive sin out, sin will drive us out." As the old saying goes, "If we give the enemy an inch, he'll take a mile."

~Nancy

Fleeting Moments of Pleasure

Emma reached her goal weight using the THM principles and has some great advice for other women struggling with the balance between liberty and bondage when it comes to certain foods that come under the label of cheating.

She says, "THM has been a real eye-opener for me. I used to look at certain foods and think that giving them up would seem like prison. But instead, it feels like freedom. And as reflect on the past, I realize I was actually imprisoned back then!

"My biggest tip is to give yourself grace. Plan a cheat now and then, but don't cheat like you used to eat. A good cheat might mean having a tiny piece of cake at that birthday party. It doesn't mean you justify a bad decision every time you have the opportunity to make one! The momentary sadness you feel when you pass a temptation by literally lasts about as long as it takes to swallow that naughty morsel. When the moment passes I always feel tremendously strong and capable of saying no to other temptations as well.

"I have learned through this journey that the joy set before you enables you to endure the loss of something terribly transient (sugar-laden cake is ever so transient!). This is not to say I never crave and cheat, but each time I don't, I feel more able to stay strong the next time."

~Serene and Pearl

We're All Guilty

Gossip disturbs me. According to many Bible verses, it disturbs God even more. "He that goeth about as a talebearer revealeth secrets: therefore meddle not with him that flattereth with his lips" (Proverbs 20:19); "A froward man soweth strife: and a whisperer separateth chief friends" (Proverbs 16:28); "Let no corrupt communication proceed out of your mouth, but that which is good to the use of edifying, that it may minister grace unto the hearers" (Ephesians 4:29).

Some people flatter you in front of your face but crush your reputation behind your back. Often we can tell who these people are by hearing how they speak of others. Maybe that's how they speak about you.

We're all guilty of gossip. By lowering the reputations of others, we might feel we are raising our own. But Psalm 101:5 states, "Whoso privily slandereth his neighbor, him will I cut off: him that hath an high look and a proud heart will not I suffer." God expects more than kind words to people in person. He expects kind words about people when they're not around. Gossip is breaking the Golden Rule: "And as ye would that men should do to you, do ye also to them likewise" (Luke 6:41).

If we don't want to be gossiped about, we shouldn't gossip.

~Meadow

eighty-seven

Stress or Rest?

Isn't Zephaniah 3:17 a wonderful promise? It reminds us that "The Lord thy God in the midst of thee is mighty; he will save, he will rejoice over thee with joy; he will rest in his love, he will joy over thee with singing." What does God mean by resting in His love?

The Hebrew word means "to be silent, to hold your tongue." The same word is translated "hold your peace" or "hold your tongue" thirty times in the Bible. When God forgives us from our sin and cleanses us with His precious blood, He remembers our sin no more. He doesn't accuse us or bring it back to remind us.

God wants us to enjoy this kind of love in our marriage relationship, too. It's so easy to accuse. It's too easy to retort back. It's easy to bring up past hurts and arguments. But does this bring rest in your relationship? No. It only brings more nervous tension. It raises the blood pressure. Instead, God wants you to rest in each other's love. Rest your tongue, too, instead of answering back to have the last say.

Other translations refer to this concept as "quieting love" (ESV); "calming love" (CEB, NLT, and WEB); and "renewing love" (NET, GWT, and RSV). These kinds of love will bring joy to your marriage.

Will you ask God to help you be silent and "hold your tongue" today? With no more retorts you'll have rest instead of stress!

~*Nancy*

A Cover-Up

The layers of lessons in this verse are many: "Ye are like unto whitened sepulchers, which indeed appear beautiful outward, but are full of dead men's bones" (Matthew 23:27). It was spoken to the Pharisees who were only about the outward appearance of godliness. Christ exposed the corruption inside. Taking physical application for this spiritual truth, we realize that only taking care of the outside of our body and ignoring the state of our inner health is also hypocritical.

Many people go to the salon once a month to get their hair and nails done. They shop for coordinating outfits and spray perfume on their bodies. Inside though, things may be in a desperate state of ruin with sky-rocketing blood sugar, fatty liver disease, impacted colons, yeast overgrowth, high blood pressure, clogged arteries, and the list goes on. Yet these bodies are painted, preened, shaved, and presented as healthy.

True health and beauty comes from within the body. Adequate protein repairs muscle and skin tissue; nourishing, healthy fats add luster to the skin, nails, and hair; antioxidants, found in greens, berries, and meats, destroy free radicals that rob our body from glowing luster; hydrating, sensibly sweetened drinks remove toxins and clear the skin.

We're not saying you should not put on makeup or get your hair done, but do it to enhance flourishing health, not to cover up decay. Take the inside-out approach.

~Serene and Pearl

God Is Protecting Us

Some might wonder why God included so many laws in the Old Testament. He went so far as to discuss clean and unclean foods, even cleansing.

It's not because God is a God of laws, it's because God is a God of love. His laws were common sense. He was protecting the children of Israel from diseases. And more and more, science proves that some foods are harmful to our bodies and that cleansing is crucial. History has shown that those who fail to follow those laws are only harming themselves.

We might know the back of our hands, but Matthew 10:30 says, "But the very hairs on your head are all numbered." It's foolish to believe God doesn't know what's best for us when He knows us better than we know ourselves.

~Meadow

eighty-eight

A Paradox

Women are a paradox of strength and softness. You reveal the anointing of softness as you nurse your baby and mother your children. You reveal your soft spirit as you speak sweetly to your husband and children. Your compassionate and loving spirit fills your home.

But you are not weak and insipid. You are filled with strength as you stand guard over your marriage, your home, and the souls and minds of your children. You are a dangerous watchdog. You do not give into the subtleties of the enemy who comes to woo you and your children into his deceptive ways. You stand strong against all desensitization. You stand true to your convictions, and you will not yield one inch to the the adversary of your soul. You stand, and having done all, stand (Ephesians 5:13).

You do not give in to defeat and despair. You do not give in to weariness. You constantly find your strength and sufficiency in the Lord your God.

Be a whole woman. Embrace fully your anointing of both strength and tenderness.

~Nancy

Are You Carried or Caring?

You move to a new town and visit a church for the first time. They're having a community meal after church and invite you to stay. "No problem!" they assure you when you mention you did not bring any food, "There's plenty to go around."

But imagine if you joined the church and kept turning up to the monthly potluck empty-handed, constantly receiving, expecting others to feed you. You'd always remain the needy newbie, relying on others to take care of you, rather than becoming a contributing member, eventually reaching out to other newbies.

Paul exhorted the New Testament church in Hebrews to grow up and move from drinking the milk of the Word to chewing on the meat (Hebrews 5:13, 14). Babies that drink milk cannot even feed themselves. They are helpless without someone else taking care of them.

Spiritually, we should not stay as babies. Jesus Christ cleanses our sin when we are born again, but then He begins molding and shaping us into new creatures through His word.

Our health journeys should not be spent as babies either. Yes, it is perfectly fine for someone to hold your hand as you begin, but if you don't find your own feet and feed yourself after a while, you'll have to be carried around by someone else.

Sadly, some people purchase our book but never read it; instead, they constantly ask others how to do the plan. Yes, there is a learning curve, but anything worthwhile in life takes some effort. Chew on some meat today!

~Serene and Pearl

Right and Wrong

"What is right if there's no wrong?" It may have been the deepest line in my poem "This Without That," which I wrote when I was much younger.

I often wonder where non-believers get their moral ideas from. If they don't believe in God's morals, what morals do they believe in? They would believe in the culture's morals, the people's morals, and their own morals—man's morals.

Perhaps a long time ago, Christian teachings were taught in schools. Everyone grew up with those teachings whether they believed in God or not. Because of their cultural teachings, anyone can respect their parents without respecting God. Anyone can honor purity, faithfulness, and honesty, because otherwise, they will shock their culture. But they don't mind if they shock God. They could have a good work ethic to impress the people around them but not to impress God.

But what happens if the culture starts taking away Christian teachings?

They would be replaced by other "morals." And it doesn't matter if they are biblically correct, because they are the world's *right* instead of God's.

What happens if the culture says, "Please yourself; you decide what is right and wrong"? Then there is no longer right and wrong.

~*Meadow*

eighty-nine

Only by God's Spirit

Zerubbabel (along with others) came back from Babylon, their land of captivity, to rebuild the temple of God. They faced difficulties, challenges, and persecution as they attempted this great building project. You too are involved in a great building program as you build a strong marriage and home. Or maybe you are seeking to rebuild. Like Zerubbabel, you find you cannot do it in your own strength.

The prophet came with a word from God to encourage him: "This is the word of the Lord unto Zerubbabel, saying, Not by might, nor by power, but by my Spirit saith the Lord of hosts" (Zechariah 4:6). I cry out these words nearly every day of my life. I cannot face all my challenges in my own wisdom. I cannot make my family members walk in God's ways. I cannot accomplish the task with my limited capacity. It is only by the moving and working of the Holy Spirit in my life and in their lives. I am totally reliant upon the power of the Holy Spirit.

Praise God for His power, which works in us mightily (Ephesians 3:20; Philippians 2:13; Colossians 1:29; and Hebrews 13:21). The prophet continued in Zechariah 4:7, "Who art thou, O great mountain? Before Zerubbabel thou shalt become a plain." Do you have mountains in your way? Through the power of the Holy Spirit, the mountains will become a plain! Claim this promise and the Word of the Lord to you.

~Nancy

Weight Loss Stalls

The THM program was not designed for fast weight loss. Your skin and organs need time to adapt and deal with toxins as they are flushed from your fat cells.

When people mention they have "only" lost 20 pounds in six months and consider quitting, we congratulate them on such fantastic progress! Natural weight loss will never be a regular figure every week. It dribbles, it drabs, sometimes it whooshes, but other times, it halts for a while as the body takes time to heal.

Paul the apostle is thought to have written a whopping fourteen books of the New Testament, and he spent a generous amount of that time telling us to press on. He knew people would feel like quitting sometimes. But what is back there for us? Nothing. Our spiritual journey is not a quick sprint; neither is our physical journey.

Pearl: *Keep your eyes on the long-term goals. My husband took five years to lose fifty pounds with THM! But he enjoyed the journey completely. He's been able to keep that weight off easily because he didn't have an agonizing experience. He didn't feel so deprived that he longed for his old eating ways. He'd sit at the same weight for months, eating his Tummy Tucking ice cream every night—then whoosh . . . down another five pounds. Be encouraged; that slow and steady turtle won the race, didn't he?* ❧

~Serene and Pearl

Mean to Me?

I used to struggle with being unhappy with myself. Even every now and then, it can still sneak up on me. But I have a strong memory of my mom saying something to me that hit me. It was a wakeup call.

"Do you know that you are being mean to yourself, Meadow? This is not you! You wouldn't be mean to other people, would you? Then why would you be mean to Meadow?"

It was hard to take because I knew it was true. I felt guilt. I felt like I had sinned. And you know what? I had. God loves me, but I didn't always love myself. It was in this way that I was being mean, ungrateful, and hateful when I knew that I was called to be kind, grateful, and loving. And although we are not called to be self-centered and are to prefer others over ourselves, this gives us no excuse to be mean to ourselves.

I don't want to be mean to me anymore. Don't be mean to you.

~Meadow

ninety

A Great Opportunity

Isn't the word "longsuffering" such a lovely word? Not so easy to put into practice, though! The word means "forbearance, fortitude, patience, and longanimity." I hadn't heard of that last word until I checked the 1828 Webster's Dictionary. It means "a disposition to endure long under offenses." Trials can go on and on. Can we keep enduring for the long haul?

We can't in our own strength, only in Christ's strength. He lives within us and He is longsuffering. This is His nature (Joel 2:13; Romans 2:4; and 2 Peter 3:9, 15).

Paul confessed, "That in me first Jesus Christ might show all longsuffering, for a pattern" (1 Timothy 1:16). Can we have this testimony in our daily life and home? Mothering is a great opportunity to show longsuffering, isn't it? And do you notice that we are also to be "a pattern"? We are an example (by word and action) to our children and all we meet. They learn by imitating us.

Embrace the frustrations and trials of life. Each one is an opportunity to reveal the longsuffering of Jesus and to conform you to the image of God's Son (Romans 8:29).

~Nancy

Neglected or Pampered

Finding the balance between these two approaches on how you take care of your body can be hard for some of us. Many women feel that if they take time to make sure they eat right, exercise, get enough rest, or put in a little effort for beauty, they are doing something that may be selfish and frivolous. These things are not spiritual enough or important on their list of priorities. They will constantly look after others—their husbands, their children, their co-workers, their friends, their homes, their purses, their laundry—anything but themselves.

While the Bible warns us against putting too much focus on outward vanity, it also mentions the beauty of the face and physical form of many of the biblical heroines. If this didn't matter at all, it wouldn't be mentioned in the Bible. Of course we should not try to be Barbie dolls or constantly seek and expect more "me time," but we are our husband's investment and our children's role model.

The Scriptures tell us in 1 Corinthians 7 that as married folk, our bodies are not our own, and we should not begrudge intimacy to one another. We also glean from this Scripture that we look after our physical bodies not only for our own purposes but also because when we said, "I do," we gave our body to someone else. Do we just let them go after a few years and not bother with basic physical upkeep?

~Serene and Pearl

God's Open Door

Every teenager gets asked if they are going to college. Some people believe in college like they believe in going to church. Some young people plan which college they want to go to before they even know what they want to study.

I have friends and family who went to college, and most of the time, it was for the best! I support the students who know what they're doing. College can be crucial for certain jobs and professions. And it is definitely helpful in many other cases. But that doesn't mean it has to be for everyone. It doesn't have to be for me.

Why am I not in college? Because I am already authoring books, because I don't really need to take a course to write a song, and because I don't see why I should be in college if I can't see myself as a surgeon or in another profession that requires it. Even so, this is the pressure that is thrown on me in my culture. The statement of my own path could be treated with a low look of disapproval instead of the supportive understanding that I have sensed God has other plans for me.

Go to college for the right reasons. Go if it's necessary for your own unique destiny. But don't go simply because that's what the world expects of you. Choose your true calling.

~*Meadow*

ninety-one

The Family God

God says in Jeremiah 31:1, "At the same time, saith the Lord, will I be the God of all the families of Israel, and they shall be my people." God planned from the beginning of time that the way He wants us to live in this world is as families, not separate individuals, but families. He even wants the "solitary" (the deserted and lonely) to be in a family (Psalm 68:6). And therefore, He wants to be the God of every family.

Is God *truly* the God of our personal family life? Would someone coming into our home immediately feel the presence of God? Are our children aware that God is preeminent in our home? Is God honored in every decision we make, every word we speak, and every action? Do we honor Him by coming together as a family each morning and evening to hear Him speak to us as we pour out our hearts to Him? Or have other things taken His place in our home?

If God was *truly* God in family homes across the nation, we would become a righteous nation. The fear of God would come into the land. We would push back the darkness of sin and deception. We would become a strong nation.

Can we allow God to *truly* be God in our family—in every moment and every situation? It starts with each individual family. My family. Your family.

~*Nancy*

Keep on Singing

Psalm 104:33 says, "I will sing unto The Lord as long as I live: I will sing praise to my God while I have my being."

From the time I could talk, I didn't stop singing. It was a real "fair dinkum" (as we say down under) habit. I sang wherever I was. My mother never lost track of me as she just followed my voice. My father would have to curb me singing at the table.

Through the years, I sang love songs to God. I sang about His goodness, hope, the beauty of creation, and happy memories. I sang about my husband and crooned lullabies to my babies. Sometimes I just hummed notes with emotions I couldn't verbalize and prayers to God my soul couldn't translate to my tongue.

Then, so slowly that I wasn't even aware of it, I slowed down until I completely stopped. Maybe it's because life is so busy, and there is so much noise in my home of nine growing children. Don't get me wrong: I am a super happy person, and the hubbub of our home life is a happy hubbub. But I recently realized that I don't sing anymore! What made me all grown up and boring? How did I lose the art of making music in my soul to where it can't help but bubble out?

Some habits are worth holding onto so I'm singing again.

What good habits have you grown out of? Maybe it's a crazy dance in a summer rain. Or the delightful habit of joyful laughter.

~Serene

Jesus Writes My Story

The day of my birthday, my friend Callie encouraged me by saying, "Jesus is the author of our lives and I know that He is writing something beautiful for you." What a lovely metaphor to say to someone who wants to be an author herself! But it wasn't until after reading Hebrews 5:9 that I recognized the Scripture: "And being made perfect, He became the author of eternal salvation unto all them that obey him."

While I am becoming an author who is writing about Jesus, Jesus is the author of authors who is writing my story! And my writings are only based on His writings. His are original. I am excited to discover the brilliant plots, the lessons, and the little details in the fresh story He writes for me. No one, not even I, will be able to think it up.

    ~Meadow

ninety-two

Will the Pages Be Blank?

What do you love to do when you get together with other believers? What do you love to talk about? Malachi 3:16 says, "Then they that feared the Lord spake often one to another: and the Lord hearkened, and heard it, and a book of remembrance was written before him for them that feared the Lord, and that thought upon his name." This Scripture is a beautiful picture of the saints fellowshipping together. Not gossiping together, but discussing God's Word and sharing testimonies with one another of His goodness and daily mercies to us.

I am always excited to learn more of the Scriptures and love to hear what others are discovering.

"What has God been saying to you lately?" I sometimes ask. Blank stares. No reply.

"What book are you reading in the Bible at present?" Once again, there is no reply.

We are always eager to talk about what is on our heart, aren't we? Therefore, if we are thinking about the Lord, don't you think we'll want to talk about Him? As we receive new understanding from reading God's Word each day, we'll be keen to share it. So why the silence?

Surely, as believers, we are not talking more about movies, concerts, shopping, clothes, and anything but God and His Word.

Will our pages in God's Book of Remembrance be blank, or are we filling them up?

~Nancy

Move On!

Deuteronomy 1:6 tells us, "The Lord our God spake unto us in Horeb saying, 'ye have dwelt long enough in this mount.'" In this passage of Scripture, the children of Israel had already experienced several victories over many enemies. With God's help they'd claimed more ground. But God wanted to give them even more. They had yet to possess the Promised Land that He longed for them to dwell in.

Have you made some health progress? Perhaps you've conquered your battle with soda. Perhaps your blood pressure is coming down. You can walk up the stairs without being winded. These are all mountain-top worthy experiences, but don't stay on Mt. Horeb. God has more for you. What's the next victory He wants to strengthen you to climb?

~Serene and Pearl

Wise as Serpents

"Behold I send you forth as sheep in the midst of wolves: be ye therefore wise as serpents, and harmless as doves" (Matthew 10:16).

Serpents and doves are as opposite as sheep and wolves. The Greek definition for serpents includes "sharpness of vision." The snake is a "sly, cunning, artful" and a "malicious person, especially . . . Satan."

It doesn't say to be "as serpents" but "wise as serpents." We must know how the wolves (or serpents) think in order to evade them, just as armies know they cannot prevail without a strategy.

Knowing enemies isn't always easy. Earlier, Matthew 7:15 warns, "Beware of false prophets, which come to you in sheep's clothing, but inwardly they are ravening wolves." If these wolves pretend to be us, how will we know? "Ye shall know them by their fruits" (Matthew 7:16). "A good tree cannot bring forth evil fruit. Neither can a corrupt tree bring forth good fruit" (Matthew 7:18).

Wolves prey on sheep. "For I know this, that after my departing shall grievous wolves enter in among you, not sparing the flock. Also of your own selves shall men arise, speaking perverse things, to draw away disciples after them" (Acts 20:29–30).

While we go as sheep preaching to the lost sheep that have become ravenous wolves, we must be careful ourselves not to become like the wolves. This is one way to be wise as a serpent and harmless as a dove.

~*Meadow*

···· ninety-three ····

Stir Up the Pot

When we find someone believing a lie, what's our reaction? When someone is going astray, what do we do? Most times, we'd prefer to say or do nothing. We don't like to interfere. We don't want to be thought of someone who is condemning or legal, so we keep quiet.

But is that what God wants us to do? Proverbs 28:4 says, "They that forsake the law praise the wicked; but such as keep the law contend with them." The Hebrew word for "contend" is *garah* and means "to meddle, to stir up." In other words, stir up the pot!

Is it loving to leave someone in deception? Is it loving to not seek to rescue someone who is going in the wrong direction? (Read Jude 23). How can we change society if we stay silent? God wants us to invade society with His truth. He wants His people to show the way. He wants us to shine His light into the darkness, not hide our light (Matthew 5:13–16).

This doesn't mean we will be condemning in our response. A great way to challenge people's thinking is to ask them questions. Ask them why they think the way they do. Ask them about their worldview. Christian and non-Christians are constantly bombarded with a secular and humanistic worldview. We have to redirect their thinking back to God's way.

Don't hide your light. And don't forget to smile at people when you confront them.

~Nancy

The Bull's-Eye

Hebrews 11:6 says, "But without faith it is impossible to please him." These words hit a bull's-eye through my heart. Without faith it's impossible! Impossible? That's a very strong word, especially when Luke 1:37 says that nothing is impossible for God!

God can't pour His powerful possibility into a vessel that isn't lined with faith. All that power just leaks out. With God it is all "Can do," yet we resist with our impossible "Can'ts." The cup that harnesses the Almighty God's strength and power is formed by the substance of faith.

What are we left with when faith is gone? Fear! This is the antithesis of faith. This four-letter word is the one thing that makes the God who can do the impossible rendered helpless in His ability to rescue us. I must believe not only in His salvation for me but also in His unfailing goodness, divine sovereignty, and all knowingness.

I must trust in His pruning and not resist the Master Gardener while He ploughs the rows of my life so it can bear fruit. With childlike faith I must lay still on the Potter's wheel while He firmly presses my hardened edges of clay and by friction molds me into His desired vessel. I must allow Him to pour into my cup whatever drink He would have me sup, saying, "Not my will, but thine be done."

A fearless life is one that pleases Him.

~Serene

Living in the Light

One of my favorite parts about flying on a plane is meeting new people, complete strangers. Instead of passing them in the grocery store, you have no choice but to sit next to them for hours at a time.

I've often prayed that God will give me opportunities to witness to people. Those opportunities are scarce when you are surrounded by godly friends and family. But when I travel, God throws these opportunities at me. He doesn't just show me the people to witness to, He *tells* me what to do by giving me a little feeling deep inside.

I talked about God to the lady sitting next to me as casually as the flight attendants were talking about the Super Bowl. I knew that she wasn't a

Christian, yet she believed in God. Somehow, I knew that I had to be patient with her and encourage her with love and kindness, while inside, I wanted to tell her what she was missing out on! Instinctively, I also knew I needed to pray for her . . . and to tell her that I would!

When you see someone who's lost in the dark, you're suddenly aware that you have been found in the light. The realization hits you more than ever. You feel gratitude that you're no longer living in the shadows, and you trust that you are strong enough to pull the other person out of the shadows and into the sun.

~*Meadow*

ninety-four

Savvy Secret

Recently I read about a wife whose husband was unkind to her and didn't want to spend time with her, choosing to spend all his evenings in other company. She went to a counselor. He didn't spend hours counseling her, but instead, gave her one simple message: "Always treat your husband with a smile."

She began to put it into practice. A few months later she returned to the counselor to say that her husband no longer sought other company but longed to be with her and treated her with constant love and kindness.

This secret works wonders for a problematic marriage; it also enhances a good marriage. Try it.

What about your children? Do they get more frowns than smiles from you? Second Corinthians 3:18 tells us that we grow into the likeness of Jesus the more we behold Him. It says, "But we all, with open face beholding as in a glass the glory of the Lord, are changed into the same image from glory to glory, even as by the Spirit of the Lord."

In the same way, your children become like the image they see on your face. Do they see a grumpy face? If so, they'll be grumpy. Do they constantly look at a smiling and happy face? If so, you'll have happy children.

Smile even when you don't feel like smiling. Soon you'll be smiling because you feel like it, and everyone in your home will be smiling, too.

~Nancy

Act Like Newlyweds

My husband and I attended a New Year's Eve function where we sat at a table with people we had never met before. About halfway through the evening, we mentioned our five children, and the couple sitting opposite us acted surprised that we had children together. They asked how long we had been married and when we told them nineteen years, the husband shook his head and chuckled. He had presumed we were newlyweds! His wife admitted she had wondered the same thing. I asked why and the man said, "It's the way you act together, how you look at each other."

My husband and I do not act like we are all over each other when we are out, but we usually hold hands or touch in some way. It's a habit we've formed. We still gravitate to one another when we are in a group of people; we enjoy conversations with others but never separate completely in a social gathering. Who could be more important to me than him?

There are many reasons we could have ended up like the typical stereotype of a bored and passionless, long-time married couple. We've gone through the same issues that most married couples have that threaten passion and intimacy: children, challenging years, health concerns, financial stressors—so many excuses to drift into relational complacency. Our strong bond is only because we choose to cultivate it every day. Just like with food, you change destructive habits with more constructive ones day —by day and yes, the results are fantastic!

~Pearl

Already Ready

Waiting for your groom is a type. The ultimate wedding is when the bride (church) and the groom (Christ) take place. But in the meantime, the bride's duty is to prepare for the big day. She doesn't know when that day will be, but she must be ready for it. At the same time, she must also live with her other duties.

Throughout every century, every decade, every year, and every day, many people believe we are in the last days. We can get clues from the book of Revelation! But that doesn't mean it's time to quit our jobs and wait around for Christ's return because we've "calculated" that time.

That's what some young girls want to do. Sometimes, they don't want to care about doing other works because their Prince Charming is supposed to arrive at any minute. The key is to have a life but also to be ready for the new one at the same time.

~Meadow

ninety-five

Stuffy or Liberating?

Philippians 1:1 enjoins us to be "filled with the fruits of righteousness, which are by Jesus Christ." Isn't it wonderful that every word that God gives us in His Living Word relates to us in our daily life? That means right *now*. It could be in your kitchen with your children or in whatever you have ahead of you today. It could mean a challenging situation, or even an overwhelming one!

What does it mean to be a righteous mother? What does it mean to establish a righteous home?

Let's get it straight. Righteousness is not legality. Righteousness is not stuffiness. Righteousness is not religiosity. Righteousness is not going around with a long boring face!

Righteousness is the life of Jesus shining through your life—through your smile, words, and actions. It comes forth from your hands and feet as you serve with joy in your home.

Righteousness is equated with joy. Speaking of Jesus, Hebrews 1:9 says, "Thou hast loved righteousness, and hated iniquity; therefore God, even thy God, hath anointed thee with the oil of gladness above thy fellows." Jesus had more joy than anyone else because He loved righteousness.

You are not called to create a "religious" home, filled with laws and regulations. You are called to establish a righteous home, filled with the joy and peace of the Holy Ghost (Romans 14:17).

~Nancy

Hug Like You Mean It

If you are married and have not yet read the "Foxy Mama" chapter in *Trim Healthy Mama*, please do. If you're single, this chapter is not for you yet. But to the marrieds, let me give you this challenge.

Next time you see your husband today, walk over to him and give him a hug. There's a hug and then there's a *hug*. Don't be quick about it . . . linger. Fill your hug with love, promise, and meaning. Let your husband know that he is wonderful to you through this hug. No, he's not perfect, but he doesn't have to be perfect to deserve your hug. He's your husband; he is precious, so you gladly give it to him.

This is one little daily habit you can incorporate to replace a more negative one. Hug like a newlywed!

~Pearl

Pray For One Another

When someone is poor, struggling, or they can't seem to find a job, we feel the need to pray for them financially. Prayer that is selfless. When someone is sick or dying, we feel the need to pray for them physically. Prayer that is caring. But over and over again, the Bible uses prayer as a request to pray for others *spiritually*. Prayer that is love—that they will know *His love*.

Paul prayed for the saints in Ephesus for their "wisdom," "revelation" and "knowledge of Him." (Ephesians 1:17). Paul and Timotheus prayed for the saints in Philippi that their "love" would "abound more and more in knowledge and in all judgment" that they would "approve" things that are "excellent," be "sincere and without offense" and be "filled with the fruits of righteousness" (Philippians 1:9-11).

Paul, Silvanus and Timotheus prayed for the church of the Thessalonians that "the name" of "Lord Jesus Christ" would be "glorified" in them and they in Him (2 Thessalonians 1:12). After warning him that Satan would sift him as wheat, Jesus himself prayed for Simon that his "faith" would "fail not," and when he was "converted" he would "strengthen" his brethren.

There are three main ways to pray for someone: financially, physically,

and spiritually. They go in the order from least important to most.
   ~Meadow

ninety-six

Drifting with the Current

We don't have to do one thing to drift with the current, do we? It happens without our doing anything. We can lay back and relax and watch the world go by.

Hebrews 2:1 (Weymouth) says, "For this reason we ought to pay the more earnest heed to the things which we have heard, for fear we should drift away from them." Drifting is an unconscious process. Westcott comments, "We are all continually exposed to the action of currents of opinion, habit, action, which tend to carry us away insensibly from the position which we ought to maintain."

Conversely, it takes concerted effort and untiring strength, conviction, and purpose to go in the right direction, which most times, is against the current of this world.

Are you living against the grain of this society? Keep standing strong. Don't be intimidated. Don't cave in to the easy way. You may receive scoffing and contempt from family members and people around you, but put your shoulders back and lift up your head. You are on God's course! Your end is "Well done, thou good and faithful servant." Your disdainers are deceived and deliriously drifting on dangerous currents.

And please, do everything in your power to keep your children from drifting in the current of this world. We as parents are responsible for this generation.

~Nancy

Help! My Church is Making Me Fat!

Pearl: My children learned to eat donuts at church! Every Sunday morning they could not wait to get to church for the donuts before Sunday School, then the Goldfish crackers, candy, and Kool-Aid during Sunday School. But it's not only the children the churches stuff with sugar and empty starches. Most church social events are centered around big helpings of sugar and empty starches. ❧

Of course we are not saying quit church! But get savvy about what to eat before and after services and at the numerous potlucks you will attend.

1. Don't go to church hungry. Have a hearty, protein-rich breakfast—maybe scrambled eggs and sausage, or choose to have one of our desserts for breakfast on Sunday morning. This way you won't feel deprived when others are eating donuts; you'll have already eaten a large piece of slimming cheesecake.
2. Keep a safety snack in your purse since after church, you may be famished. A few nuts or some cubes of cheese will satisfy. Or slip in a low-glycemic protein bar.
3. Time for a potluck? Take a protein-based dish and an on-plan dessert that will wow others as well as satisfy your own sweet cravings. There are usually plenty of salads to choose from to help fill your plate.

Your meal may not be perfect, but it will be a long way from being destructive to your overall health.

~*Serene and Pearl*

Walk in Respect

"Rid me, and deliver me from the hand of strange children, whose mouth speaketh vanity, and their right hand is a right hand of falsehood: That our sons may be as plants grown up in their youth, that our daughters may be as corner stones, polished after the similitude of a palace" (Psalms

144:11, 12).

There are so many children who have no sense of respect. They speak empty and useless words of nonsense, and base their words on lies. We see this attitude portrayed in the movies, TV shows, and even in the families we associate with today.

But sons should be growing with a life that is full of purpose, not lacking meaning. Daughters should be improving the home, not tearing it apart.

~*Meadow*

As for Our Family

Micah 4:5 says, "Though all the peoples walk each in the name of his god (whatever captivates their attention), as for us, we will walk in the name of the Lord our God forever and ever."

Do you want this confession to be the testimony of your family? I want it to be our affirmation: "As for the Campbell family, we will walk in the name of the Lord our God forever and ever."

What a great affirmation for you and your children to speak out loud each morning, "As for us (put in your family name), we will walk in the name of the Lord our God." Perhaps you could all say it together at breakfast time. Or find the most appropriate time, especially when your husband is home with the family.

What a privilege it is to walk in the name of the Lord God. What a responsibility to take His name upon us, our family, and all that His holy and awesome name represents. As we make this a family confession and testimony, it will remind us to conduct our lives in a way that will bring honor to His glorious name.

How long are we to walk in His name? Forever and ever. It is not only for your children now. God wants each continuing generation of your family and my family to continue walking in His ways. Pray not only for your children but also for the coming generations.

~*Nancy*

Fullness of Rest

Observing a day of physical rest is not only a healthy habit established by God; it was also instituted as a picture of His provision and plan for us to find perfect rest in Him. Striving on our own is offensive to a God who wants to hold and carry us.

Jesus came to fulfill the Sabbath, and He is our true rest, even beyond a particular day or list of rules. Whether we are busy at work or sipping lemonade on the porch, we can experience the fullness of rest and deeply breathe in the air of Heaven that dissolves every earthly stress.

When I choose my fears over His rest for me, I spit on His precious gift of Sabbath rest. How silly of me to abstain from busy work yet still fret over something insignificant. Jeremiah 17:21 says, "Thus says The Lord: 'Take heed to yourselves, and bear no burden on the Sabbath day, nor bring it in by the gates of Jerusalem; neither carry forth a burden out of your houses.'" Jesus is my Sabbath rest, and I profane Him by bringing all manner of burdens through the gates of my heart and carrying them around in my home.

Jeremiah 17:23 heightens my challenge: "But they did not obey nor incline their ear, but made their neck stiff, that they might not hear nor receive instruction." I want to confess along with Isaiah 50:5: "The Lord God hath opened my ear, and I was not rebellious!"

~Serene

Dad Is My Hero

My Mom is the main cook in our family. And she is good. But on the rare occasions when my Dad cooks, it is special, even if the cooking isn't good. Actually, you might not call toast cooking. But that was my Dad's specialty. Burnt black, toast—my siblings and I would beg for it! We'd run to the kitchen as the smoke called our name! Mom could never make toast like Daddy. I'd complain how hers was always perfectly brown. I liked how Daddy's was black.

This was all before *THM*, of course. But it's a memory I cherish. When I look back at my childhood memories of my Dad, it's not the presents he gave me that are the first that come to mind (although, I have those memories, too). It's when he made burnt toast.

Our dads are not our heroes because they buy us ponies and wear a cape like superman. Our dads are our heroes because they are our providers, our instructors, our caretakers, and simply because they're our dads.

Maybe it was more than my love of burnt toast that got me excited. Maybe it was also because I love my Dad.

~*Meadow*

ninety-eight

Standing Guard

Obadiah 11 talks about foreigners entering into the gates of Jerusalem. As mothers, we have to constantly guard our home. We must watch for anything "foreign" sneaking through the gates of our home.

The "foreign" is all around us. God doesn't want to take us out of it; He wants us to be shining lights in the midst of it. Jesus prayed, "I pray not that thou shouldest take them out of the world, but that thou shouldest keep them from the evil" (John 17:15).

However, although it is all around us, we must be on guard that none of the "foreign" enters our home. Our home is to be a sanctuary from evil—all that is opposite to God's standard, His Word, and His heart.

The Adversary looks for any opening he can find to intrude into your sanctuary. Guard your gates. Guard your home on all four sides. By intercession and prayer, put a hedge of protection around your home (Job 1:10).

Give no foothold for the enemy. Allow no estrangement in your marriage. Don't allow any worldly spirit to come in through the media. Be ruthless against the enemy. First Peter 5:8, 9 says, "Be sober, be vigilant; because your adversary the devil, as a roaring lion, walketh about, seeking whom he may devour."

Let's have the same testimony as Nehemiah when he confessed, "I purged out everything foreign" (Nehemiah 13:30 NLT).

Read these Scriptures also: Deuteronomy 7:25, 26; Psalms 144:7, 8, 11–15; Lamentations 4:12; Ephesians 5:11; and 6:10–13.

~Nancy

Poisonous Attitudes

Food, exercise, and rest are foundational principles for health, but they do not stand alone. Fear, bitterness, resentment, hate, anger, deep grief, and other intense emotions can contribute to poor health. Proverbs 17:22 tells us that "a broken spirit drieth the bones."

It is not healthy for our spirits or our bodies to lick wounds of hurt, to harbor grudges, or to hold onto unforgiveness. Our bodies thrive or wither under our own thoughts. Nursing negativity and letting it take deep root is creating the right environment for fatigue, depression, and yes . . . disease. Proverbs 12:16 NIV says, "the prudent overlook an insult." Let it go!

~Serene and Pearl

Wisdom at Any Age

Several verses teach that with age comes wisdom. Proverbs 16:31 says, "The hoary [gray] head is a crown of glory, if it be found in the way of righteousness." Titus 2:3 says, "The aged women likewise, that they be in behavior as becometh holiness, not false accusers, not given to much wine, teachers of good things." And Job 12:12 says, "I said, days should speak, and multitude of years should teach wisdom."

We should all be seeking to be more like our elders in the way of wisdom. But does this mean that only our elders inherit this gift? No. Even children can have wisdom. Ecclesiastes 4:13 says, "Better is a poor and a wise child than an old and foolish king, who will no more be admonished." And 1 Timothy 4:12 says, "Let no man despise thy youth; but be thou an example of the believers, in word, in conversation, in charity, in spirit, in faith, in purity."

We are to respect our elders. With more years come more experiences and more wisdom. On the other hand, if our elders don't stand in the ways of God, a child or youth who does has even more wisdom than they do.

~Meadow

ninety-nine

The Best Prescription

With one little member of your body, you can light a fire for God in the hearts of everyone in your home or set them on a course of destruction (James 3:2–12). With one little member you can minister life or death to those you speak to each day (Proverbs 18:21). With one little member you can build up your marriage or destroy it (Proverbs 14:1).

With one little member you can change the atmosphere in your home, melt your husband to pieces, determine the destiny of your children, and inspire and encourage everyone you meet.

You know what it is, of course. Your tongue.

Proverbs 16:24 says, "Pleasant words are as an honeycomb, sweet to the soul, and health to the bones." Positive and lovely words actually make your bones healthy. What comes out of your mouth will either fill you with life and vitality or make you miserable and in poor health.

The Hebrew word for "health" is *marpe*. It means "a medicine, curative, therapeutic and healing, and a source of vitality." It's the same word in Proverbs 12:18: "The tongue of the wise is health (marpe)."

It's the same again in Proverbs 15:4: "A wholesome (marpe) tongue is a tree of life." God wants your tongue to be a healing tongue—healing wounds, hurts, insecurities, resentments, and estrangements. Your healing words are the best doctor's prescription you can give to your family members. They work much better than drugs!

Ask God to fill your tongue with loving, joyful, positive, and healing words today.

~Nancy

Talk Like You're Falling for Each Other

I was happily minding my own business in a bathroom stall at Walmart when someone in the stall next to me answered her phone. It was obviously her husband, and she discussed in sharp, curt tones what she'd decided to pick up for dinner, then hissed at him unkindly about not being late to their son's football practice. Then an impatient "Gotta go," and that was it. No goodbye, love you, or talk soon.

I felt very sorry for her husband. I almost wanted to give her a knowing, disapproving look as we washed hands at the same time. But then I had to remind myself of the Scripture about judging others. No, I did not often hiss at my husband or hang up the phone on him, but if someone heard our regular private conversations, would they think we were a marriage in quarrel or in love?

When we fell for each other, I was never naggy, bossy, or demeaning to him. My tone did not come across as frustrated or dull with indifference or boredom. But I'm sure the woman in the stall next to me didn't start out talking to her husband in this manner either.

I determined to keep this question in my head when it came to conversations with my husband: "Would I talk to him like this if we were falling for one another?" This simple question changed the tide of my marriage.

~Pearl

Faithful Wounds

Tough love isn't just tough for the people receiving it; it can be tougher for the people giving it. When you give what they need but don't want, you risk losing their love. It's a sacrifice. But tough love is *true* love. It's putting their needs above yours, which is the need of having their love.

A long time ago, Shakespeare talked about tough love in one of his plays when Hamlet said, "I must be cruel only to be kind. Thus bad begins and the worse remains behind." An even longer time ago, Proverbs 27:6 talked about tough love by saying, "Faithful are the wounds of a friend; but the kisses of an enemy are deceitful."

A wise person might realize this immediately. A thoughtful person might later. And an ignorant person might never. Yet it's a necessity. But if the one enduring the tough love realizes that the reason they are surrounded with smoke is because you were putting out a fire, that the reason you gave them a blow was because you were saving them from a fall, that the reason you sacrificed their love is because you love them enough to do so, then they may gain a greater respect for you than they have ever had before.

~Meadow

···················· one hundred ····················

A Sweet Perfume

What is the atmosphere like in your home? Is it filled with bickering, arguments, criticisms, and complaining? Or is it filled with the sweet presence of Christ? God wants us to live in an atmosphere of His sweet presence just as He wanted His priests to live in the aroma of a sweet anointing in the tabernacle. The recipe for the incense in the holy place was to be made of sweet spices that were to be tempered until they were pure and holy (Exodus 30:34–38).

Second Corinthians 2:14 (WEB) says that Christ "reveals through us the sweet aroma of his knowledge in every place." Did you notice that it says "in EVERY place"? That means your home. That means in your kitchen. That means when the baby is crying, the toddler is having a fit, the pots are boiling over on the stove, and your husband is demanding your attention.

It doesn't matter what is happening in your life; Christ lives in you and His attitude is sweet! Therefore, when you yield to His Spirit, you will be sweet. You can't do it in your own strength, but only as you acknowledge His sweet presence in you.

I love J. B. Phillips' translation: "Thanks be unto God who leads us, wherever we are, on his own triumphant way and makes our knowledge of him spread through the world like a lovely perfume! We Christians have the unmistakable 'scent' of Christ."

Can people instantly recognize Christ's scent when they are with you?

~Nancy

All Creation Sings

God loves singing and music. Singing ministers to our souls, those around us, and especially the One who created our voice. God wants us to sing when we are happy, sing when we are sad, sing when we have won the victory, and sing when we are in the wilderness. He wants us to make a joyful noise, even when it is a sacrifice to praise.

God wants us to sing aloud. Sing amongst the people. Sing amongst the nations. Even sing when you're alone. Psalm 149:5 says, "Let the saints be joyful in glory: let them sing aloud on their beds." God so loves these melodies of communication from His creation that He has imprinted music in nature.

First Chronicles 16:33 says, "Then shall the trees of the wood sing out at the presence of The Lord." Isaiah 44:23 says, "Sing, O ye heavens; for the Lord hath done it: shout, ye lower parts of the earth: break forth into singing, ye mountains, O forest, and every tree therein: for The Lord hath redeemed Jacob, and glorified himself in Israel." Luke 19:40 says the stones will cry out if we hold our peace and don't praise Him.

Recently a scientist-composer found that by using a special record player on a cut tree trunk, each ring was musical. Each tree played a different tune and every ring for every year was unique with a new song of praise. How much more does God want to hear your songs of praise? They are precious in the ears of God.

~Serene

Life Endeavors Should Not Be "Whatever"

While driving on day, my mom told me how she felt about a song we were listening to the on radio. The song portrayed life that was empty, boring, meaningless . . . and simply, godless. "It's this day and age," my mom stated, "they're just like, 'Whatever.'"

I knew my mom wasn't just talking about the characters in the song. She was talking about the culture in general.

This inspired me to write a country song. But when you pay attention, you will see that this song has a deeper message. When the girl in the song realizes that she can no longer be with the guy who doesn't care about anything—including her—she explains to him the reason in the chorus:

It's not that you're good; it's not that you're bad.
It's not what you've got; it's not what you lack.
It's your whole life endeavor.
You're just like, "whatever."

The message is that we live in a culture that can't tell the difference between good and bad. They're lukewarm. But instead of having our whole life endeavors be like "whatever," we should live each day with a passion.
    ~*Meadow*